You're On Your Own

D1540313

You're On Your Own

How Policy Produced Britain's Pensions Crisis

Peter Morris
Alasdair Palmer

Civitas: Institute for the Study of Civil Society
London

First Published September 2011

© Civitas 2011
55 Tufton Street
London SW1P 3QL

email: books@civitas.org.uk

ISBN 978-1-906837-31-0

Independence: Civitas: Institute for the Study of Civil Society is a registered educational charity (No. 1085494) and a company limited by guarantee (No. 04023541). Civitas is financed from a variety of private sources to avoid over-reliance on any single or small group of donors.

All publications are independently refereed. All the Institute's publications seek to further its objective of promoting the advancement of learning. The views expressed are those of the authors, not of the Institute.

Typeset by
Civitas

Printed in Great Britain by

Berforts Group Ltd
Stevenage SG1 2BH

Contents

Authors

Peter Morris worked in the finance sector for 25 years. In 2010 he wrote a report about private equity for the Centre for the Study of Financial Innovation. He can be contacted at morrisp1@aol.com

Alasdair Palmer is Public Policy Editor of the *Sunday Telegraph*, email: alasdair.palmer@telegraph.co.uk

Acknowledgements

The authors would like to thank the following, as well as others who prefer to be anonymous, for their time and other assistance: Andy Bell, Patrick Connolly, Maggie Elliott, Robin Ellison, Max Hastings, Michael Johnson, Con Keating, Paul Lee, Tom McPhail, Mark Robson, Robert Rowthorn, Andrew Strange, everyone at Civitas and two anonymous referees. It goes without saying that none of the above should be assumed to agree with any of the report's content. All views and any errors are the responsibility of the authors alone.

Foreword

Millions of people have been overcharged by the pensions industry and will end up with retirement incomes that are as much as 20 per cent lower than they might have been, and in some cases 75 per cent lower. Peter Morris and Alasdair Palmer have skilfully shown how this has been allowed to happen step-by-step over the last 30 years.

Public policies were intended to allow the vast majority of people to take personal responsibility for their income in old age by increasing savings and enhancing personal choice. The authors show that the results have been the opposite: saving has fallen; and instead of increasing people's capacity to control their own destiny, policies have produced 'scepticism, bewilderment and confusion'.

From 2012 the National Employment Savings Trust (NEST) will start to operate. Qualifying employees will be those initially earning between about £5,000 and £33,000. Employees will contribute four per cent of their annual earnings; employers will add a further three per cent; and the government will add an additional one per cent. NEST will manage individual pension funds and make a low annual management charge of 0.3 per cent per annum. Each contribution will also be subject to a once-only initial charge of 1.8 per cent. The Pensions Commission of 2002 estimated that saving at this level over a typical working life, and with similar charges, would increase the retirement income of the 'median' earner by 50 per cent.

The main weakness of NEST is that annual contributions will be capped at a very low £4,200. The chief reason appears to be a desire to appease the pensions industry, which would lose revenues. However, pension providers have behaved in such a self-serving spirit in the last couple of decades that they deserve no sympathy. Morris and Palmer contemplate increasing the limit to allow more people to protect their pension, but it would be possible to take an additional step. Why not allow existing pension funds to be transferred into NEST? This would allow people currently paying annual management charges of 1.5 per cent or more to escape the clutches of the pensions industry. The end result would be that private pension providers would only be able to attract pension contributions from customers if they were able to beat the terms offered by NEST. This is not an impossible hope. Some American mutual funds already make an annual charge of under 0.3 per cent, often without any initial charge.

The choice for the Government is simple. It needs to ask whose interests it values most. Is it more concerned to placate the pension companies or is more interested in giving everyone a real chance of an independent, commercially-sound income in retirement? The members of a free people deserve the chance to provide for old age through honest work and saving during their working life. Yet, because of the pension fiasco of the last 30 years, many older people face the prospect of being beholden to the passing moods of political leaders for their income. It's no way to live.

David G. Green

Introduction

Old age isn't so bad, when you consider the alternative.

[Attributed to Maurice Chevalier]

On 1 March 2011, the National Pensioners Convention headed a pensioners' lobby of Parliament. The demonstrators were protesting against the government's decision to change the rate at which the state pension increases. It has been linked to the Retail Price Index—but from April 2011, it will be linked to the Consumer Price Index. This will not stop the state pension from increasing: it will simply diminish, by about 0.8 per cent, the rate at which it increases.

So imagine what the reaction would be if the government were to announce sweeping changes to the rules on pensions which would have the following results:

- Private sector employers reduce their contributions to their employees' pensions by two-thirds

- Millions of people save less than half as much as they used to for their retirement

- Millions of people are overcharged by the pensions industry

- Millions end up with retirement incomes that are as much as 20 per cent lower than they would have had, and for some, incomes are 75 per cent lower

In fact, this is precisely what has happened to private sector UK pensions over the last 25 years.[1]

And yet amazingly, there haven't been any protests. The British people have accepted, with almost no complaint, changes whose effects are to leave millions of

1

them not marginally worse off in retirement, but in some cases 50 per cent poorer or more.

One of the reasons for the lack of protest is that almost no-one outside the pensions world seems to have fully realised what has happened. If the financial crash of 2008 was a disaster that happened so suddenly it was impossible to miss, the pensions catastrophe has unfolded so slowly, and over so many years, that its effects have been difficult for most people to notice. It is like a degenerative disease whose devastating consequences take years to become apparent, and whose onset and development is so slow that a sufferer may not notice any difference in capacity until years after diagnosis. But the consequences are no less dire for being slow to manifest themselves.

The length of time that it takes for changes in pension provision to become apparent have lulled people into thinking that nothing bad has happened. We hope that if you read this report, you will be jolted out of that response.

Private pensions in Britain assume great importance because the basic state pension has always been set very low. Today, with the exception of the pension paid by the Mexican government to women, the British state pension is the lowest of any OECD country.[2] Successive British governments have taken the view that individuals should, as far as possible, be reliant for most of their post-retirement income on the savings they have built up during their working lives. We show in this report that the problems have not been with that principle, which we think is the correct one for any government to follow. The problems derive from the way it has been implemented.

The results of botched and misguided attempts to make most of us more responsible for our own post-retirement income represent a long-term catastrophe for most people. Twenty-five years ago, work-based pensions in the private sector were, for the most part, both reliable and generous. In return for saving 20 per cent of your annual income, you had the promise of an income in retirement that would bear a healthy relationship to what you earned while you worked: many people saving under such schemes were entitled to pensions of two-thirds of their final salaries.

The same is emphatically not true of most of the pension schemes in the private sector today. These schemes do not promise any level of post-retirement income at all. They are likely to result in incomes that are very significantly lower than those that would have been provided under the old system.

Not everyone is going to be affected. Those who are very rich, or who are very poor, may not notice anything much. But for the great swathe of people in the middle who have saved for their pension relatively modest amounts over the course of their working lives, old age is going to be far worse than they anticipated. It will still be better than the alternative—but probably only just.

There is one other group that will escape the damaging effects of the change in the way pensions are provided: those who work for the public sector. At present, most of those who work for the public sector are entitled to a guaranteed pension of a healthy percentage of their final salary. Take a civil servant who retires on a salary of £60,000 and then receives a pension of around £40,000. To receive a pension of comparable size from a personal pension, someone in the private sector would have to build up savings amounting to well over £1 million— which, without winning the Lottery, is inconceivable for most people who retire with a salary of £60,000 a year. So one way of looking at the generosity of state pensions is to say that the government hands its favoured servants the equivalent of assets worth many hundreds of thousands of pounds, and in some cases, worth over a million pounds—a sum which it would be almost impossible for anyone, except the very richest, working in the private sector to save.

The gap between the pensions given to those who spend their lives working for the public sector, and everyone else who works in the private sector, is enormous and getting bigger, and it will eventually have to be tackled.

Public sector pensions and their future, however, are not what we investigate here. In this report, we will show that the policies on pensions adopted by governments over the last 25 years have had effects opposite to the ones intended: instead of increasing saving, they have diminished it; instead of increasing people's under-standing of what they need to do to achieve an adequate pension, they have sown scepticism, bewilderment and confusion; they have loaded pensions with additional, often unnecessary costs; and they have led to a very serious fall in the level of retirement income that people can expect.

We'll explain:

- What has happened to private sector pensions

- Why it has happened

- What it means

- How changes to pension policy could improve the situation in future

Three figures summarise the story we will be telling in this report, and we will return to each of them. The first

4

shows the dramatic fall in the number of people with pensions that guarantee a post-retirement income amounting to a fixed percentage of the individual's salary. These schemes are called 'Defined Benefit', or DB schemes—we'll explain more about the terminology in Chapter 2.

Figure 1:
Active members, UK private occupational pension schemes

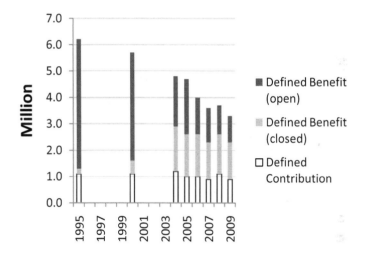

Source: Office for National Statistics, *Occupational Pension Scheme Survey 2009*, published October 2010. The blank columns appear because before 2004, data was not compiled every year. Note these figures exclude individual (non-company) pension arrangements.

The second figure (p. 6) shows the dramatic increase that has already happened in the number of people who are saving in schemes that do not provide or promise any definite income in retirement; and the even more dramatic increase that is expected in the next ten years.

These schemes are known as 'Defined Contribution' or DC schemes.

Figure 2:
Total UK private sector defined contribution pension savers

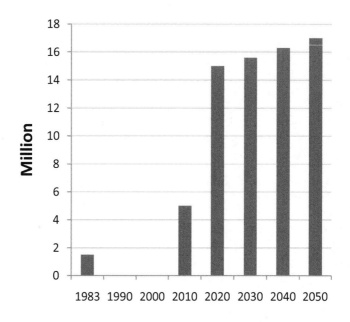

Source: Pensions Policy Institute, 'Retirement income and assets: outlook for the future', February 2010. The 1983 figure is the authors' estimate. Comparable 1990 and 2000 figures not available. Unlike Figure 1, these figures include individual pension arrangements.

The third figure (p. 7) shows how much worse off some of those who save in the second kind of scheme (DC) may be compared with those who are lucky enough still to have one of the old-style DB schemes.

Figure 3: Illustration of the difference between DB and DC pension outcomes

From DB to DC (including lower saving)

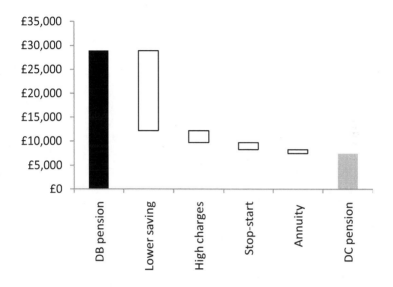

Source: authors' calculations, see pages 29-41. These figures illustrate the different pension outcomes that are possible for two hypothetical individuals who start work in 2011 on the same salary of £20,000 and work for 40 years.

To explain the dramatic changes represented by these three figures, the next chapter examines how pensions are funded. Chapter 2 explains the difference between DB and DC schemes in detail, and why DB is superior to DC. Chapter 3 looks at the reasons why DB schemes are nonetheless being replaced by DC schemes. Chapter 4 examines financial decision-making; the final chapter asks how the situation can be improved.

1

How Pensions Get Paid For

There is a great deal of complex jargon surrounding pensions. It sometimes appears that the whole topic has been made deliberately obscure and complex. The effect has been to make it almost impossible for anyone who is not a pensions expert to understand what is involved.[1] So in an attempt to make the whole issue more comprehensible, we're going to go back to first principles.

Funding and Sustainability

The two central issues for any pension system are: who is going to pay for it? And how will they raise the money to do so?

No pension system will be sustainable if the money it pays out to pensioners is larger than the money that is, or has been, paid in. If more is paid out to pensioners than has come in to fund those payments, then at some point, there will be no money left to pay out, and there will therefore be no more pensions.[2]

That is the situation which every pension fund— whether it is your own individual pot, or a collective pension fund for everyone—has to avoid. It is critical to the design of any viable pension scheme, whether for an individual or a society, that it ensures that the money available to pay pensions does not run out while the people who depend on them are still alive.

So any pension scheme has to identify the people who are going to pay for pensions, and to provide some explanation of how they will raise the money to do so: if those who are supposed to be going to pay aren't actually willing, and able, to pay, then the pension scheme will collapse. That is why, in our view, the issue of how pensions are funded has to be considered in tandem with the matter of individual incentives to save and pay for pensions: the extent to which individuals are prepared to save and pay for pensions, whether their own or those of others, will ultimately determine how much money there is available to fund any pension for anyone.

At the level of public policy—the rules that will apply to everyone in a society—there are only three ways of answering the question: who will pay for my pension?

- I can pay for it all on my own

- other people can pay all of my pension

- the payment can be shared between me and others

In determining pension policy, the Government has to decide which of those three options will deliver, in a sustainable way, the best (or perhaps the least inadequate) pensions for most people.

A society's ability to pay pensions to some of its members depends on the willingness of those who are working and producing wealth to agree that a portion of that wealth should be transferred to those who are in retirement. Pensioners always have to be supported by the labour of the current working population, so the central issue is to justify an individual pensioner's claim over a portion of the surplus that the working population produces—and in a way that reliably and sustainably persuades the working population to hand over enough of the resources they are producing to fund pensioners appropriately.

One basis for such a claim is that, during his working life, an individual saved enough money to mean he has a contractual entitlement to resources to support him in retirement. He has, that is, built up assets which can be used for his pension, and this is the source of his claim over a portion of the product generated by the working population.

Another basis is that he has a claim on those resources just by virtue of reaching retirement age: whether or not he saved anything is irrelevant. Those in work are simply obliged to fund his retirement.

Clearly, those two different claims have radically different effects on how far people in work are motivated to transfer resources to pensioners.

We'll call the system under which my claim to those resources is based solely on the assets I have built up by saving during my working life, 'private pensions'.

The system where my claim is unrelated to whatever I have saved during my working life, and where others are obliged to provide me with resources regardless of how much I have saved, or indeed whether I have saved anything, we'll call 'collective pensions'.

The two extremes—a society which allows *only* private pensions; or alternatively, one which allows *only* collective pensions—need not detain us very long. They have been rejected by almost every modern government, including that of the UK. And for very good reasons. The central difficulty with a policy of requiring each individual to pay the full costs of their own pension is that it means that those who, for whatever reason, fail to save enough, or at all, receive no pension whatever. In theory, and perhaps in practice, once they can no longer earn their living by working, they will have no income, and they will be left to fend off starvation by whatever means they can.

The cruelty and humiliation inherent in that outcome means it is one which no modern society thinks acceptable: every country with a developed economy seeks to avoid it by ensuring that there is some pension, or equivalent income, available even to those who have failed to save anything for themselves.

Furthermore, a private system based on each individual funding and managing their pension arrangements on their own, can create difficulties for those who save throughout their lives. Suppose you have invested your pension savings in the stock market, and in the week before you are due to retire, the stock market loses half or more of its value. Then through no fault of your own, the value of your pension will fall to half, or less, of what you expected. That may mean it is no longer enough to enable you to live decently. You may even fall into a position barely distinguishable from those who have saved nothing at all.

Awareness of both of those problems is one reason why the opposite extreme, a system based on purely collective provision, where individual savings are irrelevant to any pension entitlement (or indeed to any future entitlement at all), can be seductive. But as with most collective monetary benefits, there is an almost-impossible-to-resist temptation to overlook the critical fact that the money for each person's pension has to come from someone. There are no 'free pensions'. We tend to think that pensions are a 'collective' benefit which can somehow be magically provided by 'the collective', without any money having to be transferred from one individual to another. But the collective has almost no money[3] over and above the money that comes from the individuals who make it up—which is why the idea that other people will pay for all of my pension is unworkable.

The central problem here is sustainability: if I know that other people will pay whatever it costs to provide me with an adequate pension, I have no incentive whatsoever to save for a pension myself. And if the rule for the whole society is *that no individual pays for their own pension*, the same will be true of every individual in the society— which means no-one will save, and that will mean there will be no saving for pensions at all, and thus no money to pay out pensions with.

In practice, every system that comprehensively severs the link between what an individual saves during his working life *for* his pension, and the amount he receives *as* his pension, is vulnerable to the charge that it is not sustainable, for those who are paying for other people's pensions are overwhelmingly likely to prefer to spend the money on themselves—which means that, sooner or later, the funding for the collective system will collapse. In theory, it is possible to tax the working generation at high enough levels to support everyone who is retired at whatever level of comfort or luxury the retirees want. But in practice, we can be sure that those working will object to being taxed at high levels for that purpose, and soon find ways to avoid paying or to change the law so they don't have to—which will bankrupt the pension system.

The fundamental principle that underlies private pensions is that the more I save for my pension, the higher the pension I am entitled to. Because any sustainable system will have to incorporate that principle, at least to some extent, every pension system that is viable in the long term will have to be based on private pensions. But it will also have to have collectivist elements: otherwise the system won't be able to provide pensions to those who are unable to provide for themselves.

Ways of mixing private and collective provision

So some of the costs of providing pensions will have to be shared. There is obviously an enormously large number of different of ways of sharing those costs. Different systems will place different degrees of emphasis on private pensions, as opposed to the collective ones, and vice-versa. In this report, we examine the way that government policy in Britain has emphasised private pensions over the last 25 years, and how that emphasis has affected the level of post-retirement income that people in Britain can expect.

At this point, however, we note that collectivism is not simply a way in which a community can provide pensions to individuals who, either through bad luck or imprudent spending, reach retirement age with insufficient savings to live on. A pension scheme, based on the private pension principle that the amount I receive is proportional to the amount I save, can be combined with collectivist elements—and if it is, there can be very significant benefits even for very fortunate individuals.

The easiest way to see this is to consider the benefits that come from sharing risks with other members of the collective fund. One risk that every pension system has to ward against is that pensioners out-live their savings. You retire at age 65. You don't expect to live for more than 30 years at the very most. So you calculate how much you can spend each year based on not living beyond your 95th birthday. But suppose you turn out to be healthier than you thought, and live to be 105. Then you will have ten years with no pension, because you will have exhausted your fund ten years before you die. This is called longevity risk, and it is why people use their pension savings to buy an annuity, which gives you a guaranteed income for the rest of your life: how much you have to pay for that privilege depends on how high an income you want, and how long you expect to live. The companies who sell annuities need accurate predictions about how long people are going to live for in order to be able to price them. The larger the group of people for which they have statistics on life expectancy, the closer the fit between the prediction of how long on the average member of that group is going to live after retirement, and how long any one individual member actually lives. Because longevity predictions can be produced more accurately for large groups than for a single individual, when you are part of a group, companies selling annuities will offer them to you at a much lower price than if you were on your own.

Belonging to a large group of savers can also help an individual avoid the risk of a sudden collapse in the value of investments. If you're on your own, you are at the mercy of fluctuations in the value of your investments, which may mean you wind up with a much smaller pension than you expected. An employee who happened to retire in March 2009 could easily end up receiving a pension only half that of a colleague who had saved the same amount and invested it the same way but who retired in October 2007—purely because the stock market fell precipitously in the year and a half between when his colleague retired, and when he did.[4] But if you are part of a large group, which has many members who are not yet retired who are paying contributions to a collective fund, the fund can continue to pay you at the level you expected even after a sudden crash. Because it receives the contributions from those who are not yet retired, the fund has enough money to do so. And it can make the payments without jeopardising the value of the next generation of retirees, because it is a safe bet that the stock market will eventually recover, and then exceed, its old value. This means that, by the time it comes to pay their pensions, the value of the stock market will have increased the value of the fund's investments to make up the loss.

It can therefore be advantageous for a scheme which is funded along individualist lines to have collectivist elements. The collectivist elements involve a transfer of risk from one individual to a group made up of many. One of the most significant challenges of pension policy is to find the best way to combine both the private and collectivist elements so as to maximise individual incentives to save for, and to pay for, pensions. The problem with 'too much' collectivism is that it inhibits individual saving, because too many think that someone else will provide—and that means there is ultimately insufficient money to pay decent pensions to the bulk of the population. The problem with 'too much' emphasis on private pensions is that it can produce the same result by a different route—as we shall explain later in this report.

The dangers of 'too much' collectivism: unfunded state pensions

We have already noted that the UK state pension is the lowest in the developed world. One reason that policy-makers have wanted to keep the state pension low is that they have shared the concerns we have just raised over how it can be funded in a sustainable way. Pensions paid from state funds are generally pensions paid for by other people's money. Although there is usually a contribution from the individual to their own pension, it typically only represents a small portion of the amount that they receive.

State pensions are usually referred to as 'unfunded', or 'Pay As You Go' [PAYG] schemes.

Why? Because they rely on the present generation of working people to pay the bulk of the cost of the pensions of those who have retired. So who will pay the pensions of the present generation of working people when they retire? The next generation of working people. But who will pay *their* pensions when *they* retire? The next generation... and so on, and so on, apparently *ad infinitum*.

The present generation of retirees gets the pensions. Those in work now—that is, the next generation of retirees—pay most of the costs. But the present generation of retirees, when they were working, paid most of the costs for pensions for their elders.

The viability of the scheme depends on the state investing enough money now to pay pensions for the next generation. Nothing prevents the state from doing this. But equally, nothing, of course, compels it to. It might do so. But it might not. In a democracy, the present generation of workers who are paying for the pensions of their elders is liable, indeed likely, to exert political pressure to diminish the amounts that are transferred from them to those who are retired. How can we, who are paying taxes now, and whose taxes are being used, now, to pay the pensions of those who are retired now, be sure that the state will keep its promise to us to pay our pensions when we get to retire? And that it will have the money it needs to be able to do so?

The short answer is that we can't be sure—we can only hope that the government will put aside some of the taxes we pay to fund our pensions. But there will always be an incentive to use most or all of that money now, to fund the pensions of those who need them now.

Breaking a promise to pay pensions of a specified level to future retirees, in order to be able to use the money to benefit those around at the moment, cannot happen when every individual provides a pension for him or herself and contributes nothing to anyone else's—and it is one reason why it can seem, in attempting to formulate policy that will maximise pensions for everyone, responsible and sensible to diminish the role played by the state pension.

Paul Samuelson, one of the fathers of modern economics, was the first to point out this problem for pensions provided by the state. He also thought that it didn't matter—provided there was consistent economic growth into the indefinite future. Summarising his own views, he wrote that 'social insurance... is actuarially unsound. Everyone who reaches retirement age is given benefit privileges that far exceed anything he has paid in... How is this possible? It stems from the fact that the national product is growing at compound interest and can be expected to do so for as far ahead as the eye cannot see. Always there are more youths than old folks in a growing population. More important, with real incomes growing at some three per cent a year, the taxable base upon which benefits rest in any period is much greater than the taxes paid historically by the generation now retired.' Samuelson concluded that 'a growing nation is the greatest Ponzi Game ever invented'.[5]

Politicians, economists, administrators and the rest of us are understandably less sanguine than Samuelson was about basing pensions on a 'Ponzi scheme'.[6] We are far from sure that one of his crucial conditions—that there are 'always more youths than old folks in the population'—will continue to hold. Population projections for the developed economies, Britain's included, show people who are too old to work productively making up an ever-increasing portion of the total. That suggests that future generations of workers will have to pay ever-higher taxes to support the pensions of those in retirement. Samuelson may have been right that consistent economic growth could enable the state to pay today's pensions with savings that were intended to provide income for tomorrow's retirees. The trouble is, we are all much less sure about that condition as well: consistent economic growth is very far from a certainty. But if we do not get consistent economic growth, at a high level, then unfunded pensions will quickly lead to a gigantic fiscal crisis.[7]

Funded pensions

That is why it has seemed a much better policy to try to ensure that the largest portion of an individual's pension is the result of his own private savings. When an individual's pension derives from his own savings, it is said to be 'funded': a pot of cash, or an asset, is built up over time by the individual, using his savings; the income from that asset is then used to pay the pension.

Funded private pensions come in two forms: Defined Benefit (DB) and Defined Contribution (DC).

Those two acronyms DB and DC sound very similar— but the things they describe are poles apart. Under-standing the difference between DB and DC pensions is crucial to understanding the problems with the present system of pension provision, which we think stem from a policy that has placed too much emphasis on individuals acting alone.

A **defined benefit (DB) pension** provides you with certainty about what your retirement income will be. It takes care of both how you accumulate your savings and the amount of income you will receive when you retire. What's 'defined' is the benefit, i.e. the pension income you will eventually receive. Typically, this income is related to your salary—either your final salary, or a measure such as the career average. If you worked all your life for one employer, you are usually in a DB scheme entitled to a pension for life, equivalent to a healthy percentage of either your final or your career average salary.[8]

Most people who pay into DB pension schemes have no idea of the mechanics of investment and annuities that lead to their pension. But that is not a problem: they do not need to. It is one of the great advantages of the DB model that, other than the fact they are saving for one, individuals who are contributing to DB schemes have no need to know anything about how their pensions work.

In a DB pension scheme, employee and employer make regular cash contributions into a collective pot. The resulting sums can be enormous: the Universities Superannuation Scheme, for instance, looks after a pot that was worth £30 billion at March 2010.

As far as employees are concerned, that's it. There is nothing more to worry about (assuming, of course, that the employer and its pension scheme remain solvent). They may or may not notice an entry on their monthly pay slips called 'pension contribution'. Most employees probably don't know how much they and their employers are contributing. Once they've joined the scheme, they certainly don't have to take any significant decisions.

The employer has all of the responsibilities for seeing that their employees' contributions are converted into suitable pensions.

To see this, imagine a company called Acme Services. Sue, who works for Acme, sensibly joined the defined benefit (DB) pension scheme it offers all its full-time employees. The pension scheme is a promise that Acme makes to Sue: if you contribute to the pensions pot in the way we've agreed, then Acme promises that when you retire, you will receive a retirement income of, say, two-thirds your final salary until you die. (If you work for Acme for less than 40 years, the payment will be adjusted appropriately.)

To keep her side of this bargain, Sue has to do nothing beyond continuing her monthly contribution to Acme's pension fund—which is itself an automatic, passive process that requires no action from her.

At the same time, Acme has made Sue an extremely long-dated, open-ended promise. If Sue lives to be 100, Acme is committed to paying her an unknown annual amount in the year 2090. That represents a truly remarkable level of commitment to Sue: companies rarely take on such commitments in their normal operations.

To understand how this works, imagine Sue joined Acme in 2010 when she was 20. She might work for Acme for 40 years before retiring in 2050. In 2010, when Acme makes its pension promise to Sue, what would Acme ideally like to know in order to work out exactly how much keeping its promise will cost? A very long list could include:

- How long will Sue work for Acme?
- If she stays with Acme for 40 years, what will her salary be in 2050?

- How long will Sue live after 2050?

- What will inflation be between now and 2050? Between 2050 and when Sue dies?

- How much will the pension scheme's collective pot earn on its investments between now and 2050? Between 2050 and when Sue dies?

Now multiply each of those questions by both the number of members the pension scheme has today and the number of members you think the scheme will go on to have throughout the next 80 years.

This illustrates that any company that runs a DB scheme takes on an enormous amount of risk, and work, on behalf of its employees. If you are Acme's shareholders, you will worry about how those responsibilities will affect the company's long-term profitability. Sue doesn't have to worry about any of that. She has a promise from Acme. In a defined benefit (DB) scheme, she knows what she's going to get. Acme is the one facing all the uncertainties and decisions.

It is all very different with a **DC scheme**.

A defined contribution (DC) pension scheme only deals with one stage in the pension process: accumulating the money for an individual's pension. How that money later gets turned into a retirement income—the size of the pension that is paid, and how long those payments last—is left open in a DC scheme.

This raises a very basic question: in what sense does a DC scheme actually provide a pension? We think a DC scheme is not really a pension scheme at all. It is more accurate, and far less confusing, to label it 'a retirement savings scheme'.

In a DC scheme, the only thing that is defined is the contribution: what goes in, the payments that come from you and from your employer. The benefit—the amount you receive when you retire—is left open. It could be large. Or it could be close to zero. When you invest in a DC pension, no-one can be sure. But as an individual saving for a pension, the only thing you really want certainty about is what sort of income you can look forward to in your retirement. And yet that is just what, on a DC scheme, you cannot have.

Furthermore, under a DC scheme it is you who has to decide how big a pension pot you'll need to receive the sort of income you think you will need when you retire; and you who has to figure out how much you will have to save now in order to have a reasonable chance of receiving it. You also have to work out how to turn your savings into a retirement income.

Suppose Acme's pension scheme is not defined benefit (DB) but defined contribution (DC). Under a DC scheme, Acme does not promise Sue a pension of any specified amount. In fact, it does not promise her anything. It may still make a contribution every month to Sue's savings for her pension. But it will be far lower than the amount Acme would have contributed under a DB scheme.

Here are the figures for the amounts companies in the UK which operate DB schemes contribute to an employee's pension, compared with the amounts that companies operating DC schemes contribute:

Table 1: Contribution to company pension schemes

% of salary	Employee	Employer	Combined
DB	4.9%	16.6%	21.6%
DC	3.0%	6.1%	9.0%

Source: PPI, 'Pension Facts', October 2010 Table 22

(Note that there is nothing inevitable about these percentages. Companies used to contribute less to DB schemes when they were less expensive to operate.[9] Equally, there is no legal or structural reason why companies contribute so much less to DC schemes. From a shareholder point of view, though, if they can get away with doing so—why wouldn't they?)

The smaller contributions of Acme's DC scheme will go into an individual pot belonging to Sue rather than into a collective one. Acme will also provide some administration services, as well as a range of funds in which Sue can invest her pot. But when it comes to the key decisions, Sue is on her own. She now faces a list of questions similar to the ones Acme faced when it was providing an old-fashioned defined benefit (DB) pension scheme:

- How many years am I going to work, at Acme or elsewhere?

- If I decide to retire in 2050, what kind of annual income will I need?

- How much will it cost in 2050 to buy an annuity to provide this?

- What will interest rates, inflation and mortality rates be between now and 2050? Between 2050 and when I die?

- How much will I be able to earn on the cash that I put in my pension pot over the next 40 years?

- What do I have to invest in to earn that?

Only when Sue has the answer to all those questions can she figure out how much she has to save each month in order to have at least a chance of receiving a pension of the amount she wants. She can't know how good the bet is: that will be determined by the value, in 20 or 30 or perhaps 40 years time, of what she invests in, and what it will cost to buy an annuity on the date she retires—and no-one can have any very clear idea about that now.

In the next chapter, we look in more detail at the difference between DB and DC schemes.

2

Why are Defined Contribution (DC) Pensions Such a Bad Deal?

Two conceptual problems with DC pensions

1. DC schemes aren't pensions

The first and most obvious problem with a defined contribution (DC) pension is that it isn't actually a pension.

Each of the first six meanings of the word 'pension' in the Oxford English Dictionary contains the word 'payment'. We think, as does almost every ordinary user of English, that a pension is a regular income. The opening words of a 1965 book on the subject put the point perfectly: 'To most men and some women a pension means a regular source of income which they hope to get when they retire from work.'[1]

But you do not get an income from a defined contribution (DC) scheme. A DC scheme provides something quite different: a pile of savings. This will be a means for you to provide yourself with an income in retirement. But until you retire, you're a long way from knowing what that income will be. You have no idea in advance how big your pile of savings will become (many people may not even realise how uncertain that is). Even if you could know in advance, you still wouldn't know what kind of income it would provide. That's because the income you get will depend on what annuity rates are at the time. Since annuity rates in turn depend on interest rates and a range of other things, forecasting annuity rates is even harder than forecasting interest rates—basically, impossible.[2]

Using the same word, pension, for both a defined benefit (DB) and a defined contribution (DC) scheme is a bit like an estate agent describing a large tent as a house. A tent has some of the characteristics of a house: it is a shelter against the wind and rain. Some tents are comfortable spaces in which to live, at least for a while. But a tent lacks the critical feature that we expect anything that can be called a house to have: durability. And if an estate agent had sent you the particulars of something he described as a house, and when you went to see it, you found yourself confronted with a tent— you'd think he was deliberately wasting your time.

There is a parallel with the situation when people are told that a DC scheme is a pension. The difference is that most people fail to notice. They think they've got a pension when actually they haven't. They think they have a house when in reality they've only been sold a tent.[3]

It is curious that policymakers have consistently failed to distinguish between Defined Benefit pensions and Defined Contribution schemes. This is not just a question of semantics. There are very fundamental differences between the two arrangements. One of them is that they are likely to produce vastly different outcomes for the people who have them.

Policymakers could have used tax incentives to encourage companies to favour DB. One incidental result would have been to make sure that people understood the difference between DB and DC. Instead, DB and DC receive broadly the same treatment when it comes to tax. At least for people who are employed outside the public sector, policymakers never saw any value in encouraging DB schemes, although these clearly produce vastly superior benefits for those who pay into them. The similar tax treatment has the effect of implicitly confirming that the two arrangements are equivalent: it helps to persuade people that it is correct to label both of them 'pensions'.

Most politicians, civil servants and regulators still belong to solid, old-fashioned defined benefit pension schemes: the one group of employees for whom DB pensions have remained largely intact are public servants. The shift from DB to DC over the last twenty years has had no consequences for their own pensions. Perhaps, had they been pushed out of DB pensions and into DC schemes, they might have investigated the effects of the change with more vigour, or even considered whether there were alternatives to it.[4] Whatever the reason, policy makers appear to have embraced the shift from DB to DC without imagining it would seriously harm overall pension provision.

2. With a DC scheme, you're on your own

A second big handicap for DC, relative to DB, can be summed up crudely in the phrase: 'You're on your own'.

Anyone trying to create a retirement income faces two main risks. The first part of the process—investing to build a pension pot—is risky because stock markets go up and down a lot: remember the example of the two colleagues on page 14, who retired only eighteen months apart. In the second step, you convert your pension pot into a retirement income. This triggers longevity risk: how long are you going to live?

Both of these risks become smaller for large groups of people. A large group of savers, of different ages, can afford to ride out stock market fluctuations in a way an individual simply cannot. Longevity insurance—just like other kinds—is always cheaper for larger groups of people. What makes a DB pension scheme such a powerful mechanism is precisely that it channels these benefits of acting collectively to its individual members.

A DC scheme turns its back on the obvious benefits of acting collectively. Individuals are left to deal with investment and longevity risk on their own. This should not be confused with simple economies of scale. A member of a large DC pension scheme may benefit from its buying power in terms of fund management charges and the like. But this is something quite different (and less valuable) than the ability to share risks. To see this, consider health insurance. Health insurance companies can offer you as a member of a large group a much better deal than you would get if you tried to negotiate a price for insuring your health care costs on your own. That's because, providing the group is big enough, the insurance company can assess the average health outcome for members of a group, and then offer you a price based on that average. But if you tried to negotiate the deal on your own, there would be no 'average' outcome: insurers would have to assume the worst about what would happen to you, and price your insurance accordingly.

By failing to share risks, a DC scheme makes those risks more expensive for each individual to insure against. Which means a DC scheme automatically ensures that individuals will receive lower retirement incomes than they would from a DB pension.

How DC can damage your retirement

Failure to share risks is the most damaging feature of a DC scheme. Over and above that, four practical factors also combine to make a DC scheme worse than DB pension:

1. Lower savings

2. High charges

3. Stopping and starting ('low persistency')

4. The high cost of annuities (reflecting uncertain life expectancy)

To illustrate the way those factors eat away at the value of DC schemes, relative to a DB pension, we will analyse the fortunes of two imaginary savers we will name Brian and Colin. They're twins. Both of them are 21 years old. Both of them take jobs in private sector companies in 2011. They both stay with their respective companies for 40 years and they earn exactly the same salary throughout their working lives. And each of them joins his company's pension plan.

The only difference between Brian and Colin is that Brian joins a big company that still offers an old-style DB pension plan.[5] Colin's employer is smaller and offers him something more typical: a DC scheme in which an outside provider offers a range of funds to all employees, while the company makes a cash contribution based on each employee's salary.[6]

Brian's DB pension means that he will receive an income of two-thirds his final salary when he retires.

How much Colin will receive from his DC scheme company is much more difficult to calculate. But here's why Colin's pension is going to be lower than Brian's:

1. Lower saving levels can reduce a DC pension by half compared to DB.

Smaller amounts get saved in private sector DC pension schemes (see Table 1 on p. 22). Contributions to DC pension schemes average nine per cent of salary, compared to 22 per cent in DB schemes. Most of the reduction is down to employers, who contribute six per cent in DC schemes compared to 17 per cent in DB schemes.

The opportunity to reduce pension contributions by almost two-thirds is one reason why employers have been so keen to abandon DB in favour of DC. In 1999 the *Economist* described how one large company tried to persuade employees to join something like Colin's DC scheme: 'Since last June, [Geoff Pearson, Sainsbury's pensions manager] has been encouraging staff to opt out of the company's final-salary pension scheme and, instead, to take out a personal pension with any of ten company-sponsored mutual funds from Fidelity and Legal & General. But only 2,000 of the group's 140,000 staff have done so.'[7] Those who opted out, we might add, will likely receive smaller pensions than their colleagues.

Let's return to Brian and Colin. It will take annual savings of about 22 per cent of his salary, over a period of 40 years, for Brian to earn a pension of two-thirds his final salary. Colin's individual pension arrangement is receiving contributions of only nine per cent of his salary. This means that Colin's pension plan will receive less than half as much cash as Brian's. All other things being equal, this naturally means that Colin will receive a pension that is only 41 per cent as much as his twin brother's. This is despite the fact that the two brothers have been paid exactly the same amount over their 40 year careers.[8]

Unfortunately, all other things are a very long way from being equal. DC plans contain three additional intrinsic disadvantages. Together, they will reduce Colin's pension by almost half as much again.[9]

2. High charges can reduce pensions by a quarter.

Many people (though not all) pay high costs in DC pension plans. In this context, 'high' means the costs are higher than necessary and do not represent good value.

The DC pension scheme Colin belongs to provides him with a range of funds to choose from. Costs on these funds vary, and are not always easy to understand; the following section shows *how* they are complicated. We use a figure of 1.5 per cent per annum to illustrate their impact; the following account shows that this is a reasonable figure to choose.[10]

The cost of investing

The costs that retail investors pay to invest in a fund come in at least five layers. Three of them are explicit, meaning that investors pay for them openly:

a) Initial (and possibly also exit) charge
b) Annual management charge (AMC)—what the fund manager charges for its services
c) Other explicit costs—third-party costs that the fund pays[11]

The remaining two are implicit. Investors bear these costs because they reduce the fund's return, but they do not pay for them openly:

d) Trading costs - visible[12]
e) Trading costs - invisible[13]

(a) and (b) are clearly, though not very helpfully, displayed. Initial charges range up to five per cent and sometimes beyond, while annual management charges can be anywhere from 0.5 per cent to two per cent and higher. Unfortunately, since the first is a one-off payment

31

and the second an annual charge, it's hard to make these raw figures mean anything. Even if you could, the picture would still be incomplete because it would miss the impact of (c), (d) and (e).

To get a better idea of the price you're being charged, you have to go to the small print—typically, something called the 'Key Features' document. Here you will find information about (c), which is usually quite small: say, 0.2 per cent per annum.[14] Adding (b) to (c) produces something called the Total Expense Ratio, or TER. As its name suggests, this figure is a more comprehensive and useful measure of the total running costs that a fund pays every year. It's not clear why fund management companies in the UK are allowed to bury this figure in the small print.[15]

While the Total Expense Ratio improves on the Annual Management Charge, it fails to capture the impact of initial and/or exit charges. To factor these in, UK funds provide another figure called the Reduction in Yield (RIY). This assumes that you own an investment for ten years and works out how much the combination of items (a), (b) and (c) will subtract if the underlying portfolio returns six per cent per annum. Investors who pay initial and/or exit charges quite commonly face a Reduction in Yield of two or even three per cent per annum.[16] At a Reduction in Yield of three per cent per annum, a retail investor is 'paying' half the gross return on her stock market investment. Imagine an estate agent getting paid £100,000 to sell a house worth £200,000!

Though buried in the fine print, Reduction in Yield is the most comprehensive measure of the 'price' of investing that is generally available. But it still misses the impact of a fund's implicit trading costs. Even fund managers' own trade association admits that visible trading costs—sunk yet deeper in the fine print— are 0.3 per cent per annum.[17] Invisible trading costs are hard to measure even for a fund manager. One authoritative study implied they could be between 0.5 and 0.9 per cent per annum.[18] Fund managers argue that all trading costs belong in a different category from the first three items. At the very least, though, they represent a 'drag' on the returns that will eventually reach retail investors.

These are some of the reasons why we say retail fund costs are complicated, and why we believe 1.5 per cent per annum is a moderate figure to choose. Many investors will currently be paying more than that.

The importance of 1.5 per cent per annum is easy to miss. Assume Colin's starting salary of £20,000 grows by two per cent a year for the next 40 years, and the cash he saves grows at five per cent per annum.[19] In 2011, £1,800 will go into Colin's pension pot and he will pay his pension fund manager just £15 in charges.[20] Fast forward 40 years. In the year he retires, 2051, Colin will pay his pension fund manager more than £3,000 in today's money.[21] But not once in 480 months will he actually write out a cheque or physically do anything to make this payment. That's because the charge comes off the top: it is deducted automatically each month from his pension pot.

Another reason for Colin not to notice the 1.5 per cent might be that 1.5 per cent seems such a small number. But Colin is going to be saving for a long time. Since the pension he gets in the end will be the result of 40 years' cumulative saving, he needs to think of the charges, too, in cumulative terms. After 40 years Colin will actually have paid his pension manager £45,000: almost half of the total of £108,000 that has gone into his pension pot over the years.

Like most people saving for a pension, Colin would be surprised to discover that his pension manager will receive such a large slice of his own savings. But this figure, too, is misleading. Yes—Colin will have paid £45,000 in charges. But because of the way the investments have been growing, even after paying these charges his final pension pot is worth £211,000. So perhaps the fees really are what those who charge them claim them to be: a terrific bargain?

The answer is: No. And here's why. What really counts about Colin's pension pot is how much it is worth in 2051. That's the main factor that will determine the size of his pension income.[22] Suppose Colin had miraculously found a way to get his pension fund managed for free. In that case, with the same investment returns, his pension pot would have ended up being worth £297,000. This compares with the £211,000 that Colin will have if he pays 1.5 per cent annual charges. The effect of 1.5 per cent charges over 40 years is to reduce Colin's pension pot by almost a third.[23]

This is a more helpful way to think about charges. But services always cost something, and in the absence of miracles, Colin won't be able to get his pension managed for free. However, he doesn't have to pay as much as 1.5 per cent. Suppose he finds a way to get his pension managed for 0.5 per cent a year.[24] What will the effect be on the size of his final pension pot?

The difference between 0.5 per cent and 1.5 per cent may seem trivial. But it most certainly is not. With everything else held constant, Colin's final pot would be worth £265,000 if he paid costs of 0.5 per cent a year, rather than 1.5 per cent. So if Colin can find a way to reduce his pension costs from the typical 1.5 per cent a year to 0.5 per cent, then his pension pot will increase by a quarter. And so will his retirement income.

This table shows what effect a range of all-in annual charges would have on Colin's pension pot:

Table 2: Effect of charges on Colin's pension pot

Annual fees	Final pot
0%	£297k
0.2%	£284k
0.5%	£265k
1.0%	£236k
1.5%	£211k
2.0%	£190k

Source: authors' calculations

This analysis of the impact of charges on Colin's pension pot has made one big assumption, namely that paying higher charges will not result in better investment performance. There is a very simple reason for this. Colin represents the average person. And it is a mathematical certainty that the average fund investor will actually do worse than the market. That's because the average fund manager will by definition deliver the same return as the stock market. The average fund investor who pays one per cent per annum unnecessary fees simply ensures that he will do one per cent worse than someone who buys a tracker fund at a 0.5 per cent annual fee.[25]

Of course, an average is only an average. Some people will do better than Colin; others will do worse. In Chapter 4 we discuss how the finance industry uses this fact to exploit people's gullibility, by suggesting that they could be among the winners. At a policy level, though, we believe the average is the right way to look at it.

3. Stopping and starting can reduce pensions by about 15 per cent.

The third reason why DC schemes lead to lower pensions is that it is much easier to stop saving in them than it is with a DB pension.

Nine per cent of Colin's salary went into the same individual pension arrangement, year after year, for a 40-year working life. But in assuming that Colin stays in the same job, and saves relentlessly for 40 years in the same DC plan, we're not making him representative of most people in Britain. Most of us tend to stop saving for extended periods, usually because we have other demands on our money—a bigger mortgage, a new car, an expensive holiday for the family, school fees... People also change jobs, and when they do, they frequently change pension plans. They also change their pension providers because they think another plan offers them a better deal. One study found in the late 1990s that roughly 40 per cent of individual pension arrangements in the UK had been discontinued ('lapsed') within four years of being started.[26]

Stopping and starting like this—in the jargon it's called 'low persistency'—is expensive. That's because pension providers often charge you the equivalent of a 'joining fee'. The longer you stay with the same provider, the more the impact of that 'joining fee' will diminish: it will represent an ever smaller proportion of your investment. But if you leave relatively soon after joining, you will have paid the sum, and you will receive very little for it. Suppose you get fed up with your existing arrangement after five years and move to what seems a better one. Doing this freezes the impact of the first group of 'joining fee' costs: rather than continually fading away, they stay at a relatively high level. And you may well have to pay a fresh 'joining fee' to sign on with your new provider.

Exactly how much 'low persistency' costs is hard to work out, because it requires so many assumptions. But in the UK, low persistency might reduce the ultimate size of a pension pot by about 15 per cent.[27]

4. Buying an annuity is expensive

The fourth factor that makes a DC scheme produce a lower pension than a DB plan involves the final stage of the process: not Colin's pension pot, but what he does with it when he retires.

Until recently, it was compulsory to use most of your DC pension pot to buy an annuity by the age of 75 at the latest. An annuity is a financial contract that pays you a fixed annual income until you die. This is the prudent thing to do, because it provides certainty. It means you (and also the taxpayer in the background) know you will not run out of cash and require additional support.

This certainty comes at a price, particularly if you are on your own—as you are when you paying into a DC scheme. When you buy an annuity, you are buying an insurance policy covering how long you are going to live. The company that sells you this insurance will naturally base the price it charges you on its actuarial tables: the probabilities that tell them how long they will have to pay the annual sum to you—that is, how long people like you are likely to live. People who buy annuities are statistically likely to live longer than average. Insurance companies know this, and price their annuities accordingly. This means you pay a higher price just because you are acting individually.[28]

Murthi, Orszag and Orszag calculate this extra cost at 10 to 15 per cent. Suppose Colin's pension pot when he retires is £100,000. He goes for the prudent option and buys an annuity. The lifetime income he gets from his annuity will be 10 to 15 per cent lower than it would have been if he had been able to share the longevity risk of the whole population. This would have been available to him if he had been part of a larger pension arrangement. Buying an annuity as an individual takes an additional 10 to 15 per cent off Colin's pension.

Note that this analysis assumes Colin is capable of identifying and buying the best annuity. In practice, thanks to the problems we discuss in Chapter 4, many people fail to shop around and do not buy the best annuity for them. Seven out of ten husbands, for example, buy an annuity that will provide no income to a surviving widow.[29] It seems unlikely that this is what all of them meant to do.

The combined effect is to reduce Colin's retirement income to just one **quarter** of what his twin brother Brian will receive. You read that correctly. If you save for a pension in a DC scheme with high charges, you are likely to receive a pension which is one quarter the amount of the sum that will be paid to someone who has earned and saved exactly the same amount as you have—but who has been fortunate enough to be able to join a DB pension scheme.

Table 3 (p. 39) summarises how the four factors reduce DC pensions.

Let's return to Brian and Colin and what they will receive in retirement. Brian knows from the day he starts work that his retirement income will be two-thirds of his final salary (if he stays at the same firm). Assuming as we did that his salary grew by two per cent each year in today's money, his retirement income in 2051 will be £28,860.

Like Brian, Colin worked for 40 years and received exactly the same salary. Simply because he belonged to a DC pension with high charges, though, his retirement income will be only £7,419.

Table 3: Four factors reducing DC pensions

	Reduction in Retirement Income
Lower saving	58%
Excessive charges	20%
Stopping and starting ('low persistency')	15%
Statistics (annuities are expensive for individuals)	10%
Combined effect	74%

Source: Murthi, Orszag, Orszag; author calculations

This is the effect of pension policies that have led to the replacement of DB pensions by DC saving schemes: many people's pensions will be a quarter of what they would have been. And yet it has happened without generating any concerted opposition, or even any significant opposition at all: we all appear to have accepted without complaint a change which is likely to give us a much lower post-retirement income. This is extraordinary: government proposals to cut pay by as little as three per cent (perhaps by raising income tax) generate anger and outrage. Yet the pension policy followed by successive governments over the past 20 years is going to lead to a significant reduction in millions of people's pensions. This will mean millions more people are unable to have the sort of retirement they hoped for. It will mean millions more live on the edge of poverty, dependent on the state pension for the majority of their post-retirement income.

Figure 4: Illustration of the difference between DB and DC pension outcomes

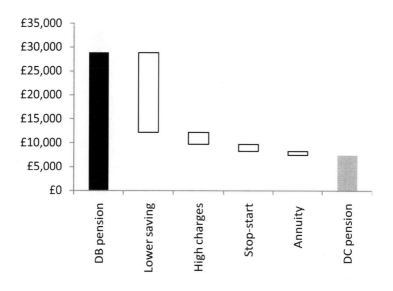

From DB to DC (including lower saving)

Source: authors' calculations. Note this Figure also appeared earlier on p. 7.

Does anyone care? They surely would if they realised exactly what is happening. We think the basic reason why the change hasn't produced widespread anger is that people have not noticed it. It has been noticed by experts in the pensions field, and extensively written about by them. But their reports have been in technical language that is hard to understand. For whatever reason, no interest group has managed to lobby Parliament successfully on this issue, and few MPs seem to be aware of it. The general population has yet to manifest any serious concern at all.

In Chapter 4 we will examine some of the reasons why people find it difficult to think about pensions in a sensible, or even just a self-interested, way. Whatever the explanation of why a policy that will cause a huge reduction in the post-retirement income of millions of people has not been met with concerted hostility, we can be sure of one thing: ignorance is not going to be bliss.

But first, in the next chapter, we trace the legislative and other changes that have led to the decline of DB pensions and their replacement by the DC alternative.

3

How Did We Get Here?

Millions of people working in Britain's private sector are going to retire with inadequate pensions.[1] Their pension prospects are certainly worse than they were 25 years ago. As we've explained, one reason for that has been the decline in the number of people who have defined benefit pensions. Another has been the decision by governments since the mid-1980s to follow the policy of ever-greater emphasis on increasing individuals' responsibility to provide their own private pensions. The two are linked: government policies that have encouraged people to make their own, private pension arrangements have hastened the decline of DB pensions.

There were some good reasons for the decision by successive governments to implement policies which emphasised ever-greater individualism in pension provision. As we explained in Chapter 1, perhaps the most pressing was to avoid unfunded, Ponzi-scheme pensions, and to ensure that individuals were more reliant on their own savings. But the process has had some very significant drawbacks.

We recognise that government policies promoting more individually-funded and managed pensions are by no means the whole explanation for the decline in the DB pension. As we show below, changes to the legal framework and accounting regulations governing DB pensions have had an important role in their rapid demise. But without the greater emphasis on individualism, the outlook for pensioners in Britain would certainly be very different, and possibly much less bleak.

It is worth noting at the outset that government policy towards pensions in Britain has nearly always tilted towards emphasising private provision. This is partly because of the political outlook of liberal individualism: the cluster of ideas centring on the conviction that individuals should be responsible for their own lives, and their own finances, and should not expect other people to provide for them—at least other people who are not family members. Those who adhere to liberal individualism insist that in principle it's wrong for resources to be forcibly transferred from those who have them in order to benefit those who do not. Gifts and other bequests are fine. But using coercion to take some people's property in order to give it to others is not.

That attitude exerted a powerful influence on British political thought and policy for much of the nineteenth century. But from the 1880s onwards, concerns about the ubiquity of poverty in old age began to generate political pressure for some form of minimal state provision for people who could not provide for themselves, something that would be an alternative to the humiliation and degradation of the workhouse—which was as much as the British state was willing to provide at the time.

The pressure was successfully resisted for 20 years by belief in the moral importance of encouraging self-sufficient individuals; in the practical necessity of deterring any form of dependence on the state (or the parish, or other people's charity); and by the conviction that it was unfair that some people should be taxed in order to pay for benefits for others who had not been prudent enough to look after themselves. Those ideas had a strong enough hold on a sufficiently large number of

Members of Parliament to prevent either Liberal or Conservative governments from introducing a state pension for those too old to work.[2]

But that pressure could not be resisted forever. There were too many British voters who thought it wrong that, through no fault of their own, thousands of men and women should be condemned to live out their lives in dire poverty. Britain was richer than Germany—yet while the German state provided a pension to some of its citizens, the British state did not.

In 1908, Lloyd George, then Chancellor of the Exchequer in a Liberal administration, finally decided that, for reasons of both justice and expediency,[3] he had to introduce a state pension. It was subject to both a means test and a test to ensure the recipient's moral character was suitable: if you had been unemployed for long periods, or were thought to be a drunkard, you were disqualified. The pension was paid only to people aged 70 or over: most people would either not reach that age, or die within a few years of it. (Life expectancy at birth for men was 48 years.) The sum paid was five shillings a week, which was below the poverty line: the average wage for a labourer was 30 shillings a week.

The state pension was set deliberately low. Lloyd George was worried about encouraging 'dependency': he and most Liberals were as convinced as most Conservatives that it would be quite wrong if any state payment were generous enough to stop potential recipients from bothering to save for their own retirement.

The thinking behind Lloyd George's introduction of the state pension has set the pattern for policy on the matter ever since. Although it is more generous now than it was when Lloyd George introduced it, the state pension in Britain has never been set at a level generous enough to allow people to live comfortably on it alone. No Labour Government, not even one in the most socialist phase of the Labour Party, has managed to introduce a universal state pension large enough to mean there is no need for it to be supplemented by further income if you want to live comfortably. The basic state pension has always been enough to ensure that old people need not die of starvation or cold. It has never been enough to secure the kind of standard of living that many people believe they should have in retirement.

So individual pensions, made up from the savings that individual workers have made throughout their working life, have been a critical part of retirement income in Britain, and have been conceived as such by policy-makers.

Private pensions, arranged through employers, preceded the state pension by several hundred years.[4] By the time Lloyd George introduced the first state pension, around one million people (roughly five per cent of the workforce) belonged to a company or other pension scheme of some kind. Just as Lloyd George and the Liberals had intended, the state pension had been set low enough to ensure that the numbers enrolled in private pension schemes went on increasing for the next 65 years: by 1967, 8.1 million people were saving in private company pension schemes.[5]

The 1970s consisted of one economic catastrophe after another for the British economy: OPEC's oil price hike, the stock market crash, the property crash, galloping inflation, and apparently endless strikes. But in many respects, the Seventies were the golden age of British pensions. Most employees were automatically enrolled in their company's scheme: joining the pension scheme was frequently a condition of employment. Almost all company schemes were defined benefit (DB)—and, as we explained earlier, DB schemes provided a number of very significant advantages, including the fact that both employees and employers made healthy savings contributions every year.[6]

Moreover, as the schemes were predominantly DB, you, as an individual saver, had no need to make any tricky financial decisions. Today, if you have a DC pension, you have to work out the answer to questions such as: How much should I save? What should I invest in? What sort of annuity should I buy on retirement? Most of us deal with those questions very badly. But in the days when most companies provided DB pensions, we didn't have to deal with those questions at all: they were tackled, and answered, by employers rather than employees. And it was the employers, rather than the employees, who shouldered the risk inherent in any form of long-term investment. As long as you kept working for the same company throughout your career, you were often entitled to a pension of two-thirds of your final salary at retirement.

All of which raises an obvious question: if DB schemes are so great, why have they disappeared so rapidly, in the way that Figure 1 on p. 5 shows?

Problems with DB schemes

It would be a mistake to claim that there were no problems associated with DB schemes, for there were several—and it was the need to solve them that led to the 'pensions revolution' which would effectively eliminate DB schemes from company pensions.

1. Lack of portability

From an employee's point of view, the most obvious problem with a DB pension is that you can't easily take it with you when you change jobs, and you lose much of your investment should you try. The critical condition for receiving a DB pension amounting to, say, two-thirds of your final salary, was that you keep working for the same company throughout your career. Conceived at a time when workers usually stayed with one employer for many years, if not their whole working lives, the traditional DB scheme effectively penalised those who, for whatever reason, changed their employers. One actuary calculated that someone who 'starts working at 20 and changes jobs only three times in his life nevertheless loses fully half his benefits in a final salary scheme'.[7]

From the 1960s, as the British economy recovered from the havoc wrought by World War Two, it became much more common for people to change jobs. Labour mobility—the ability of people to move from declining industries or companies into prospering ones—came to be seen, correctly, as essential if Britain was to have a dynamic economy. DB pension schemes needed to be adapted if they were to be compatible with a mobile labour force.

2. Vulnerability to inflation

The second problem with DB schemes was their vulnerability to inflation. As the economy began to grow rapidly, inflation started to become a serious difficulty, and the value of payments from DB pensions shrunk rapidly. Here's why. Suppose a DB plan promises to pay you two-thirds of your final salary. That amounts to a fixed payment of (let's say) £100 a week. If inflation runs

47

at five per cent a year, and you live for 15 years after retiring at 65, your pension will have shrunk to less than half its original value by the time you die. (In real terms it will be worth £46 a week.) During the 1970s, the average rate of inflation was over ten per cent a year, and for one year it ran at nearly 25 per cent. Inflation at that rate rapidly destroys the value of DB pensions. People got sufficiently concerned about it that legislation was passed to require that DB pensions increased with inflation, although only up to a level of five per cent. That was enough to make DB schemes much more expensive for companies to provide, but it still didn't provide protection against inflation rates higher than five per cent.

3. Demographics

DB schemes' third problem was a straightforward question of demographics: people were living ever longer. That meant that a company providing a pension had to go on paying it for longer, too. The maths is simple but deadly. People were still retiring at the same age, so they worked for the same number of years and made the same cumulative contribution to the pension 'pot'. But because they lived longer after retiring, they ended up drawing more pension income out of the pot than they used to. Someone had to make up the difference. That's why demographics were making it more expensive for companies to provide a DB pension.

4. Legal and accounting ambiguities

Finally, DB schemes contained some potentially trouble-some ambiguities. In legal terms, it was unclear who the cash in the scheme belonged to. This didn't really matter as long as nothing unusual happened. But as the British economy became more dynamic and competitive, the unusual became more usual and this led to complications. Suppose a company went bust, for example. If it did not have enough cash to fulfil its pension obligations, would those pension promises be met? Could a company be compelled to keep its pension pot full, just in case?

It was complicated even when a company had more in its pension fund than was needed to honour its pension obligations. To whom did the surplus belong? The consensus was that it belonged to the company and its shareholders rather than to its pension-contributing employees. That meant that the company could become the target for corporate raiders who would buy the company specifically in order to grab its pension surplus.

Pension accounting rules were as vague as the legal ones. This made it hard for people to know exactly what was going on with the pension scheme, which in turn made it hard to value a company. Again, in the relatively easygoing post-War environment this didn't matter so much. But the stock market's ever-increasing obsession with measurement and 'shareholder value', which gathered strength beginning in the 1980s, meant that the accounting ambiguity, too, was unlikely to survive.

Solutions to the problems with DB schemes?

Late 1991 saw the mysterious death of the flamboyant and fraudulent publisher and press baron Robert Maxwell. The reaction to his death and its aftermath created pressure to address many of the issues surrounding DB schemes.

Maxwell had exploited the accounting ambiguities and opacities inherent in the DB pension schemes his companies operated to transfer cash from the pension funds so as to prop up his failing commercial empire. In effect, he stole a total of £453 million from his employees' pension funds. When it became clear to him that he could not keep his larceny secret any longer, Maxwell committed suicide, leaving his companies in chaos and their pension funds in disarray, and unable to pay out the sums to which hundreds of employees were entitled. Maxwell was a powerful figure, fêted and feared by politicians, and trusted by most of those who worked for him. That he could have stolen from pension funds was a huge shock and gigantic scandal.

1. Changing the legal framework

The Government responded in June 1992 by setting up the Pension Law Review Committee under Professor Sir Roy Goode. His job was to make sure that there would never again be another pension theft of the kind Maxwell had perpetrated. His diagnosis of the problem was that 'there is no comprehensive legal framework governing occupational pensions.' So Sir Roy set about creating one.

He wanted to ensure that DB pensions always delivered the pensions they promised, and his report was instrumental in changing what had been a vague 'best efforts promise' on the part of companies providing pensions into a hard and fast contractual obligation.

Before the Goode Report and the legal changes it initiated, if a company's financial circumstances deteriorated significantly, it could negotiate with its employees to pay only a portion of the pensions it had promised. Sir Roy removed that option, on the basis that employees' pensions deserved more protection when the company providing them went bust.

In theory, that was a wholly laudable idea. But in practice, the most obvious result was that it became much less attractive for companies to set up or maintain DB pension schemes, for doing so committed them to a set of contractually enforceable obligations, the size and extent of which they could not calculate in advance. That was bad enough. It was made worse by the fact that traders could use it to claim that the company had vast debts, in the form of its pension obligations, that it would not be able to honour.

It meant that, to employers, defined contribution (DC) schemes looked much more attractive than DB ones, for with DC schemes, the employee shoulders all the risk. With DC schemes, the employer - who does not manage the employees' pensions, nor invest them, nor have to register them as a debt on the company's balance sheet - has almost no obligations at all.

2. *Changing the accounting rules*

There was also great pressure from accountants and others to change the accounting rules that governed pensions. Sir Roy was not responsible for that pressure. But it stemmed from the same anxiety that motivated his legal changes: the worry that the existing rules were sufficiently ambiguous to allow companies running DB schemes to conceal the extent of their pensions liability.

In November 2000, the UK's Accounting Standards Board replaced Statement of Standard Accounting Practice 24 [SSAP 24] with a new rule: Financial Reporting Standard 17 [FRS 17]. The old pension rule had been very forgiving. It gave companies a great deal of flexibility on how they recorded their pension scheme's investments and promises. They could use that flexibility to avoid sudden changes in the value of those pension investments and promises—which was very important, because the sudden jumps or falls in value could wreak havoc on the company's balance sheet.

The new pension accounting rule removed that flexibility. And the effect on DB schemes was the same as the Goode Report's recommendations: it made it far less attractive to companies to provide them. The two changes together undoubtedly accelerated the demise of DB schemes, not least because they spawned more than 8,000 pages of regulations—every detail of which companies had to comply with. Several large companies, including British Airways and Dixons, explicitly blamed FRS 17 for forcing them to close their DB pension schemes.[8]

On pp. 62-68 we examine in more detail the effects of the changes in the rules governing pensions schemes.

Some people blame the demise of DB on another late-1990s policy change: the 'infamous tax raid on pension funds' by Gordon Brown in 1997.[9] Brown's tax changes certainly did not help, but they were not the primary cause of the demise of DB schemes, not least because they were basically neutral as far as these were concerned: they did not give employers a significant new incentive to close them, nor employees an incentive to leave them. The tax increase on pensions might arguably have provided a disincentive to make pension contributions on the part of employees, but it is totally implausible to claim that 'had the dividend tax credit [which is what Brown abolished] remained intact, the retirement crisis which Britain now faces would never have happened'.[10] As Evan Davis pointed out in the course of a more balanced discussion, 'there were enough other, bigger things going on that did more damage'[11]—we identify those bigger causes in this chapter.

The Conservatives' radical changes to pension policy

Just as significant for the nature of pension provision in Britain, however, were the radical policy changes introduced by Mrs Thatcher's administration. Those changes were devoted to producing much more individualism, and much less collectivism, in the provision of pensions: they allowed individuals to leave company pension schemes altogether, and set up their own personal pension plans. The effects of that policy were to be enormous, and almost wholly bad.

1. The political context

The changes to the legal framework and accounting rules would not be completed until 2000. In the mid-1980s, the problems with pensions were perceived to be very different. Margaret Thatcher's Conservatives had been elected for the second time in 1983 with a huge Commons majority and a mandate for radical change. The Conservatives were committed to re-shaping Britain's economy by cutting taxes, diminishing the number of companies in state ownership, and 'rolling back the frontiers of the state' to give greater freedom, and responsibility, to individuals.[12]

Thatcherite Conservatism had many values in common with nineteenth-century liberalism: an emphasis on the importance of individuals 'standing on their own two feet'—or at least all of those who were capable of doing so —and not being dependent on state benefits or any other kind of aid or charity; a belief in the effectiveness of the free market, both as a mechanism for delivering prosperity, and as a means of disciplining behaviour; and a profound scepticism, both about the benefits that could be achieved by using the coercive powers of the state to achieve economic or social goals, and the justice of doing so.

The Thatcherites had a deep hostility to collectivism in all its forms. Mrs Thatcher gained notoriety (even greater notoriety than she already had) in 1987 when she was quoted as saying 'there is no such thing as society… There are individual men and women and there are families and no government can do anything except through people and people look to themselves first.'[13] Although she later claimed she was misquoted, it accurately summed up her case against the political policies, and the ideologies, which insisted it was legitimate to force individuals to make sacrifices in order to benefit 'society'.[14]

2. The Conservatives' pension reforms

The Conservatives decided to reform pension provision in 1985. Consistent with their anti-collectivist convictions, they wanted to increase each individual's responsibility for making their own pension arrangements and to diminish the role of the state pension. The previous Labour Government had introduced the State Earnings Related Pension Scheme (SERPS) in 1978. It was an additional state pension, run by the state on the collectivist model: everyone who did not specifically opt out was automatically enrolled into a scheme which involved higher national insurance payments, but which was intended to provide a pension for each worker amounting to 25 per cent of their final salary.

Norman Fowler, then Secretary of State for Health and Social Security, wanted to abolish SERPS.[15] Almost certainly correctly, he thought that it would turn out to be unaffordable, because it was not properly funded: the increased national insurance payments would come nowhere near to covering the additional costs of the higher pensions that SERPS promised. He also believed that SERPS was based on a 'collectivist' mistake that would sap individual responsibility and make people more dependent on the state. Just as Lloyd George had done, he thought that there were good reasons for keeping the state pension at a basic minimum. Anything above that basic minimum should be a matter for individuals: they should be free to buy from the market as much (or as little) additional pension provision as they wanted. But central government should not be the provider, or do it all for them.

In order to make it possible for individuals to make their own pension arrangements, Norman Fowler proposed introducing something which, up until then, had only been available to the self-employed: personal pensions independent of any company scheme. Personal pensions would obviously solve one of the problems with DB schemes: their lack of portability. By making the individual responsible for his own investments, they would also solve the problem that, as a member of a company DB scheme, you had to trust your employer to honour their pension promises. As we shall see, if personal pensions solved those difficulties, they also created a new set of problems which turned out to be much worse.

To encourage pension saving and investment, the new personal pensions would receive the same tax-breaks as existing company schemes. Personal pension plans would, it was hoped, achieve three policy goals at the same time. They would increase labour market flexibility by providing a fully portable alternative to company DB schemes. They would increase individual freedom, by giving individuals the responsibility for making their pension arrangements—a freedom that SERPS restricted, at least in the sense that automatic enrolment took responsibility away from individuals, and the state did not allow anyone to choose how to invest the savings they were being forced to make for their pension. Finally, personal pensions would increase the soundness of the public finances. The personal pensions would be attractive enough to ensure that large numbers would opt out of SERPS in order to make their own pension arrangements. That, in turn, would diminish the amount of tax-payers' money that would have to be spent on subsidising SERPS. The fiscal benefit would not be immediate—in the short term, they would increase rather than diminish government borrowing—but 20 years down the line, the savings promised to be enormous.

The new pension scheme was not, however, justified by the Government in terms of the money it would save the next generation of taxpayers. It was justified by the greater freedom that it would give to individuals now. Given that fact, it is something of a paradox that Norman Fowler's initial plan was to make investing in a personal pension compulsory for everyone in work. But both he and Mrs Thatcher were convinced that they would never be able to gather sufficient political support for the abolition of SERPS unless the private pension provision that was supposed to replace SERPS was made compulsory.

So that was the plan—until Nigel Lawson, then the Chancellor of the Exchequer, got his hands on the project.

Nigel Lawson objected on two grounds to making it compulsory for everyone to take out a personal pension. The first was cost: the new personal pensions would be given tax relief at the same rate as the existing company pensions. If personal pensions were made compulsory, everyone would receive the tax break on their contributions—and the resulting cost to the Treasury would be colossal. Lawson calculated that it would increase the Public Sector Borrowing Requirement [PSBR] by £1 billion in the year 1988-89, which would mean that there would be no reduction in the PSBR at all, and in fact an increase in it. But one of the Government's most important priorities was reducing the PSBR—and it was certainly more important than reforming the pension system, the fiscal benefits of which would not be felt for 20 years.

Lawson's second objection was political. The Conservatives, he insisted, were 'the Party of individual freedom'. Moreover, he noted that 'different people had different views about how much pension provision they required... to make the taking out of a particular level of private provision compulsory was wholly contrary to our political philosophy'.[16]

The self-employed, who did not pay in to SERPS, and who were a key constituency for the Conservatives, would—if forced to enrol on the compulsory personal pension scheme—have to pay, on average, an extra £200 a year each. As Lawson pointed out, it would of course be interpreted as a tax rise.

Lawson told the Cabinet that to proceed with compulsion would 'be more than a banana skin: it would be evidence of an electoral death-wish'. His mastery of the relevant statistics, and his hammering of the ideological issue, meant that he eventually persuaded Mrs Thatcher and the rest of the cabinet to abandon the plan to make private pensions compulsory.[17] Consistent with that 'freedom agenda', the Act that appeared on the statute book prohibited firms from making it a condition of employment that workers joined the company's occupational pension scheme. The compromise was that SERPS (which, like the rest of the Cabinet, Lawson wanted to abolish) stayed. But its value was reduced, from a pension of 25 per cent to one of 20 per cent of final salary.[18]

3. The effects of the Conservative reforms

The principal aim of the Conservative reforms was to increase each individual's 'freedom and responsibility' for making their own pensions arrangements. That would, it was thought, achieve two results. It would reduce the burden of paying for pensions on tax-payers, by shifting a significant part of the existing burden from the state to individuals saving for their own retirement; and it would mean that the pensions that people arranged for themselves would be better suited to their needs and preferences, so everyone would be better off.

Neither of those results followed. The net cost of personal pensions to the taxpayer during the first ten years was estimated by the National Audit Office to be about £10 billion.[19] But much more significantly, the effect of increasing individuals' freedom and responsibility for making their own pension arrangements had a catastrophic effect on saving and on pensions. Now that enrolling in company pension schemes was voluntary, rather than compulsory as it had been in the past, the number of new workers who signed up dropped by half.[20] In arguing for giving individuals the freedom to invest in their own pension funds at whatever level they chose, Nigel Lawson had taken the view that if they decided not to invest anything at all, that was their choice, and it was not for the state to interfere with it or 'correct' it. That, he maintained, was why the state should not allow firms to make enrolling on the company pension scheme a condition of employment: people had to have the freedom to choose not to save if that's what they wished to do. But, as we shall show in the next chapter, there is a great deal of evidence that many of the people who failed to sign up for company pension schemes had actually not made any decision at all. Rather than indicating a deliberate choice not to be part of the company scheme, it was often an indication of their ability to procrastinate: to put off making difficult decisions in the deluded belief that they would soon get around to them.

That said, large numbers unquestionably did take the decision to save by buying a personal pension. Indeed, the number of people who opted to buy personal pensions was far larger than expected. The Government had expected about half a million people to take out personal pensions within the first couple of years after they were introduced. In fact, 3.2 million people opted for a personal pension within the first year. By 1993, five years after they were introduced, people had set up a staggering 5.7 million personal pensions.[21]

The trouble was, many of them invested in pension products that, far from being better suited to their needs and preferences, were much less suited to those needs, principally because they would result in much lower pensions.

The Thatcherites were so convinced of the beneficial effects of the free market that they thought that competitive pressure alone would be enough to ensure that the companies providing personal pension plans offered only low-cost, good value products. So the legislation contained no restrictions on the charges that pension providers and salespeople could impose on their products. Why bother with regulations to enforce low charges? The market would ensure that charges were kept as low as possible anyway!

But in the event, the market failed to deliver that beneficial result. In fact, the result was the opposite of what ministers had intended: companies offering personal pensions imposed large charges on them, the effect of which was to reduce the value of pensions very significantly.[22]

The legislation didn't even include a requirement that transferring from an occupational scheme to a personal pension plan should be in the best interests of employees. The Prudential insurance company, which was initially one of the main providers of personal pensions, produced a booklet that informed potential customers that 'if you are already a member of a company pension scheme or will soon be eligible to join one, you will probably feel it best to stay with your company scheme.'[23] That was a statement of the obvious. Did ministers welcome it? They did not. Their initial reaction was to complain that the Prudential was 'undermining [the government's] pension policy'.[24]

The Conservatives seem to have been genuinely surprised at the actual result of introducing personal pensions: in all, about one million people were found officially to have been sold 'inappropriate pension products'.[25] The vast majority of them had been given bad advice, which they wrongly trusted to be in their best interests, as opposed to the best interests of the sales-people giving it. Miners, teachers, nurses and police officers had very good pensions, to which their employers contributed generously, and which would enable many of them to retire on healthy proportions of their final salary. But many of them were persuaded to switch to personal pensions where there was no contribution at all from their employer, and where the fees, commissions and other charges levied by the pension providers and their agents would take 25 per cent of the individual's savings.

One representative from the pensions industry told us how salespeople from his and other companies specifically targeted mining villages on the grounds that it would be easy to convince many of the miners that they would be better off in a personal pension scheme. In fact, most of those who were sold personal pensions were much worse off. A typical example was a miner who bought a personal pension in 1989 and retired five years later. Under his personal pension, he was paid less than half what he would have received had he stayed in his original occupational scheme. The figures are as follows: his personal pension paid him a lump sum of £2,576, plus an annual pension of £743. His occupational scheme would have given him a lump sum of £5,125 plus an annual pension of £1,791.[26]

On 27 June, 2002, the Financial Services Authority (FSA) announced that it would soon finish reviewing 1.7 million individual cases where mis-selling appeared to have taken place. That was almost one third of the 5.7 million personal pensions that had been sold by 1993.[27] The firms that had mis-sold pensions eventually had to pay a total of £12 billion in compensation to the individuals they had persuaded to buy 'inappropriate' products. The costs of examining all those individual cases added another £2 billion to the total costs of what was, up until the banking crisis of 2008, Britain's most costly financial debacle.[28]

In the next chapter, we will explain why some buyers of pension products can be, and still are, easily exploited by the people who sell them. At this point, we simply note that the buyers of pensions frequently did not act in their own best interests, and the sellers, in the main, did not offer them products which enabled them to do so. The idea was that 'privatising pensions'—encouraging people to manage and fund their own pensions, investing their own money after choosing the best option from competing pension providers—would lead to better pensions for everyone. But that idea has been as thoroughly falsified by experience as any idea can be.[29]

The effects of accounting rule changes on DB schemes

There is no point in having the best regulation in the world, if there are no schemes left to regulate.

'Pyrrhic Victory? ' Cass Business School, 2005[30]

An illustration of why pension accounting matters

Imagine you own a company. One basic way to measure its value is to calculate the difference between what it has (its assets), and what it owes (its liabilities).

The company you own is very simple. It has wound up all its business operations. All it consists of now is a DB pension scheme. The scheme has only one remaining member: a retired employee who receives an annual pension of £10,000. The scheme's pension pot consists of £11,000, sitting in a bank account. Since the only thing in the company is the pension scheme, both the company and the pension scheme have the same value.

Suppose this pensioner is terminally ill, and will certainly die in one year's time. Then the accountants can easily work out what your company owes: it owes £10,000 pounds to its one employee. It has £11,000 in the bank. So the company is worth £1,000 (assets of £11,000 minus liabilities of £10,000.)

Figure 5: Defined Benefit pension surplus / deficit (Simple illustration)

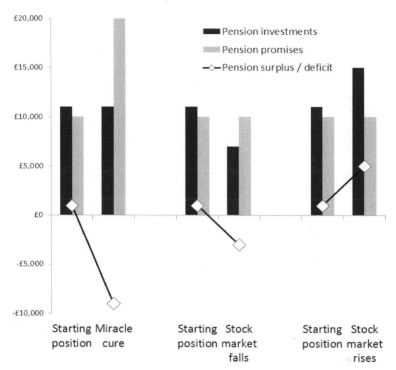

Source: authors' calculations

But this value can suddenly change. Suppose a miracle cure is invented for the pensioner's illness, which means his life expectancy doubles from one year to two. Then your company will have to pay him £10,000 for two years rather than one. That means its liabilities have increased to £20,000.[31] But your company still has only £11,000 in the bank—which means your company's value has plummeted from plus £1,000 to minus £9,000.

It's not only the value of your company's liabilities (promises) that can fluctuate. So can the value of its investments. Suppose you had taken your scheme's money out of the bank and put it in the stock market— and the stock market then fell by 30 per cent. Now the scheme's assets would no longer be worth £11,000. They are only worth £7,700. Even if there's no cure for your one pensioner, the value of your company has gone negative again—its promises are bigger than what it has to pay them with, to the tune of £2,300. Alternatively, the stock market might go up rather than down—say, by a half. Now—hey presto!—the pension scheme's investments are worth £15,000 and its surplus has risen from £1,000 to £5,000.

It should start to become clear why the shareholders and managers of large companies began to feel that DB schemes caused more anxiety than they were worth. Because the legislation turned DB pensions into a cast-iron contractual promise, providing them started to generate unquantifiable risks to the company's solvency. Developments and changes which shareholders and managers could not control, and which lay outside their control (such as sudden falls in the stock market), could turn a healthy balance sheet deep red.

The effects of FRS 17 on DB pension valuations

In 2007 the UK had about 8,500 private sector defined benefit (DB) pension schemes.[32] The Pension Protection Fund [PPF] tracks about 6,500 of them on a regular basis, in an index confusingly called the PPF 7800.

In mid-2007, all of the PPF 7800 pension pots together contained about £850 billion of investments. Meanwhile their pension promises were valued at about £700 billion. This meant that UK companies collectively had a surplus of £150 billion, i.e. about 21 per cent more cash in their pots than they theoretically needed.[33]

Less than two years later, in early 2009, a £150 billion surplus had turned into a £210 billion deficit. Suddenly, companies had about 21 per cent *less* cash than they needed. By December 2010 the schemes were back in the black (just): the schemes had £983 billion in the pot, against £961 billion of promises: a surplus of £22 billion, or two per cent (Figure 6).

Figure 6: PPF 7800 surplus / deficit, 2003-2010

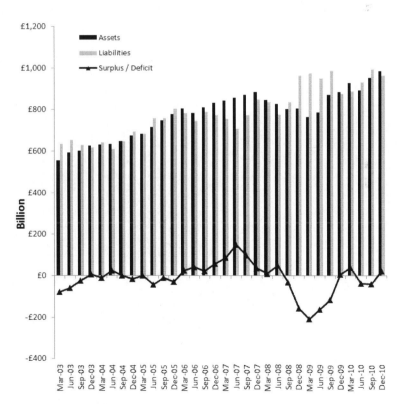

Source: Pensions Protection Fund

Aggregate figures can hide important details. It turns out that about 4,000 (almost two-thirds) of the companies in the index are in deficit. The figures for these companies by themselves are just as volatile. But their combined pension pots have never once in the last seven years had enough cash to meet their promises—at least as far as FRS 17 is concerned (Figure 7).

Figure 7: PPF 7800 schemes in deficit only, surplus / deficit, 2003-2010

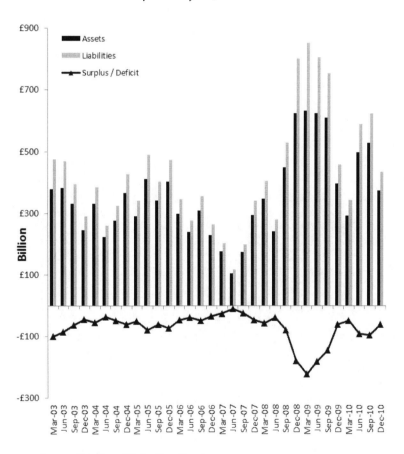

Source: Pensions Protection Fund

The pictures show how confusing, and misleading, the accounting can be. Opponents of FRS 17 would say these numbers are virtually meaningless. For the last seven years these 6,500 companies have been getting on with their business, whatever it is: making steel, designing microprocessors, supplying frozen meals to Tesco. Yet the pension accounting suggests there was a £360 billion fall, almost randomly, in their combined value between June 2007 and March 2009.

Supporters argue that at least FRS 17 provides a number that is consistent and clear. Now that the law has made pensions contractual, a pensions promise really is a promise—even if it does stretch 60 years into the future. The people who have made that promise—a company's shareholders—are entitled to be told today's 'best guess' about what it might be worth. The old accounting made it possible to shove problems under the carpet, which might store up bigger problems in future. FRS 17 advocates claim that everyone knows that the new 'best guess' is only an estimate, so it would be foolish to get too hung up about it. In any case, they say, markets are wise enough to 'look through' (i.e. ignore) the figures.

Critics ask what the point of having a measure is if you're not supposed to trust it. They say that analysts and others will use it as a basis for valuing companies, no matter how many caveats are attached to it. They say the only certainty about today's 'valuation' of promises stretching 60 years in the future is that it will be wrong. And here the critics must be right.

These details barely scratch the surface of the pension accounting debate, but it is surprising how violently experienced and otherwise sober professionals can disagree about something as fundamental as this. We suspect pension accounting probably does need to change, and that its errors are yet another symptom of the last generation's obsession with free markets.[34] For the moment, it is enough to understand the part that accounting has played in the demise of DB schemes.

4

Why We Make Bad Choices on Pensions

In 1988, when the Conservatives introduced personal pensions, they expected the results to be beneficial. Personal pensions were seen as simply an extension into the pensions field of the Conservatives' most successful policy to date: privatisation. Selling off inefficient state enterprises such as British Telecom and British Airways generated enormous gains in both productivity and consumer satisfaction: prices came down; the efficiency with which services were delivered went up. Privatisation was taken up and recommended by the World Bank: the Conservatives' policy would be copied across the world.

The dominant economic theory[1] said in 1988, and still says now, that individuals who trade freely in a competitive market will produce the best outcome for everyone—even though each individual aims only at maximising his own self-interest. While no advanced society has ever operated a perfectly free-market system, the capitalist economies have been much closer to that ideal than the socialist ones. And the failure of the socialist economies to produce anything like the prosperity of the capitalist economies is very powerful evidence of the benefits of having a market economy. Letting private companies and individuals negotiate over the prices of goods and services, rather than having them set by the state, proves its value daily in the millions of transactions between people who buy and sell everything from fruit and vegetables to cars, cinema tickets and houses.

The Conservatives, and many economists, thought it would be no different with pensions. Economic theory repeatedly insisted it would be in the interest of firms from the finance industry, competing with each other for the custom of people who wanted to invest savings to provide a pension, to come up with products that would fulfil consumers' needs. As a consequence, costs would come down and consumers would get more of what they wanted for their money. The market would work its magic—a magic which would, in reality, merely be the result of producers of financial services, and the people who want to use them, being able to trade freely with each other for mutual benefit.

As the previous chapters have shown, what has happened has not conformed to the predictions of the dominant economic theory. Instead of people providing for their own futures in a better and more efficient way, the number of people saving for a pension that will produce a known income during retirement has fallen dramatically. More than seven million over the age of 25 are not contributing to any private pension at all—which means, given the inadequacy of the state pension, that they are on course for an extremely impoverished retirement.[2] Millions of people in Britain are going to retire with no financial assets whatever.[3]

Furthermore, those who have chosen to invest in a private pension have been very badly served by the financial industry: the pensions they have been sold will, for the most part, deliver much lower pensions than consumers were led to expect—and certainly much lower than they would have received had they been able to stay with the work-place schemes that were common prior to

70

1988. Outright criminal fraud by sales executives and financial advisers has caused a great deal of suffering, but fraud has not been the major problem: the major problem has been the routine recommendation by sales executives and financial advisers of investment strategies that are legal, but which have or will deliver very poor results for the investor. There has been at least one very significant mis-selling scandal[4], which eventually required the industry to pay compensation of over £12 billion to those who had been sold products that it was clearly not in their interest to buy. And many, perhaps most, of the products being sold as private pensions still involve the sellers taking advantage of consumers' irrationality. Twenty-five years after personal pensions were intro-duced, competition has begun to reduce the costs of investing in a personal pension to the consumer—but not to anything like the extent that was expected. In most cases, costs remain too high.

What's different about a pension?

How has any of this been possible? The market in most consumer goods and services—cars, restaurants, compact discs, airlines—works more or less as the theory says it should: competition between producers reduces prices to consumers, and enables consumers to satisfy their pre-ferences more efficiently than any alternative system. What is different about financial services? What has gone wrong?

Die-hard adherents of the dominant economic theory might reply that nothing has gone wrong. The falling rate of saving merely shows that people don't want to provide for their old age: rather than save during their years of employment, they would prefer to be poor when they retire. That's their choice: it reveals what they want.[5]

We can be reasonably certain that this is not what it shows, for every time they are asked, the overwhelming majority of people insist that they do want to save for their retirement. The one thing people never say is that they are looking forward to being poor when they are old.[6]

When economists predicted that increasing each individual's responsibility for making their own pension arrangements will mean better (or at least, not worse) pensions for all, they did so on the basis of a number of assumptions. One of those assumptions is that each of us is rational, in the following sense: we know what we want; we can work out how to get it; and we can, and do, proceed to perform those actions which will achieve the result we want. We assess the options open to us using all the available information, rank them according to the extent to which they will provide us with what we want—and then act accordingly.

The trouble is that, when it comes to choosing the sorts of investment that will deliver what we want in the way of pensions, most of us are not rational in that way. This may seem an implausibly strong claim, which is perhaps why it did not occur to policymakers in 1988. We can make choices that are sufficiently rational when it comes to purchasing cars, fridges, ice creams, meals at restaurants or plane tickets: the market in these products functions as the model says it should—it delivers products that consumers want at prices they can afford.

So what happens with pensions? Why are they so different?

The time horizon

The first thing that makes a pension investment different is the length of the time horizon. A pension investment involves a commitment to save over a period of a minimum of, say, ten years. To receive a pension that amounts to a reasonable portion of your pre-retirement income, you need to save for 30 years or more. A pension is a product where it is hard to tell whether or not it has delivered what has been promised until the end of that long period. That makes it quite different from almost any other consumer item. When you buy a car or a fridge, an ice-cream or a meal at a restaurant, you know almost instantly whether you have got what you wanted: if you didn't, you can complain, get your money back, or at least make sure you never buy the product again. In short, you can learn from experience, and adjust your future purchasing decisions accordingly.

It is much more difficult to make that judgement when you are buying something that requires a commitment from you over decades. Saving for a pension is typically a life-long commitment, which means we each only get one opportunity to experience its benefits and costs. We can't learn from our own experience, because by the time we get to retirement age, it is too late to start again. So if we discover, once we've retired, that we haven't saved enough, there's not much we can do about it. We are stuck with the consequences of our earlier choices.

That's quite unlike the situation with most products, where learning from experience is critical to making the rational choice: the choice that most completely satisfies your preferences. It means that there is a serious problem about applying the economist's model of 'rational decision-making' to pension-saving. We don't know, and can't find out, a precise answer to the question: How much should I save for retirement?—until we get to retirement and discover whether the amount we actually have saved is too much or too little.[7] We may think, at the age of 40, that we know that we want a pension when we retire at 65 amounting to, say, two-thirds of final salary. What we don't know is whether it will be 'worth it', now and for the next 25 years, to forego the purchases we want to make in order to save enough to produce a pension of that amount. The difficulty inherent in finding out now whether having a bigger pension at 65 is going to be worth the sacrifices in consumption that it will require means that it is very hard to know what the right decision is.

The impossibility of learning much from your own experience when it comes to buying a pension may help to explain why it's so hard for many individuals to save enough to provide a reasonable pension for themselves. We don't know what will be enough or too much; and many of us react to that uncertainty by finding it impossible to make any decision at all—which means we don't save anything. How important is saving for a pension compared to the other things we need to spend our money on now, such as a new car, a holiday, the education of our children? Many of us are not sure what the answer to that question is, and it means we can't make a decision about how much to save. Is that irrational? It does not have to be. But it guarantees the outcome which no-one wants, which is that many people haven't saved enough by the time they get to retirement to ensure an adequate retirement income.[8]

The problem of getting accurate information

The difficulty of deciding how much you ought to save now in order to provide an income you will think adequate when you retire, is compounded when the only pension option available is a defined contribution (DC) scheme. How much a DC scheme will pay out on retirement depends on how successful your stock market investments are. Furthermore, as Chapter 2 has shown, it can be difficult to identify exactly what fees are being levied on your investment, and how they will diminish its value over time. People generally have a low level of interest in doing the mathematical calculations required for sensible financial planning, and are not very good at them.[9] Instead of doing the maths, we have a tendency to trust what we're told by advisers, and to rely on our own willingness to hope that things will work out well[10] — which is not a sensible way of ensuring that they do.

Procrastination and its effects

We also have a tendency to put off making a big decision such as investing in a pension or changing the way we invest in one. Procrastination about matters we find intimidating, confusing, or just not very interesting—all of which can describe attitudes to pensions—is very common. MORI asked people which they would rather do: change a dirty nappy, or organise their personal finances? Ninety-four per cent responded that they would rather change a dirty nappy.[11] With attitudes like that, it is not surprising that many people fail to plan properly, or at all, for their own financial futures. We don't do what is in our own self-interest, even when we know perfectly well where our own self interest lies.

Procrastination explains why many people who want to save do not do so; it also explains why people do not change their pension arrangements, even should they discover that they don't amount to a good deal for them—

which they probably won't, because they procrastinate about making the decision to assess those investments.

The failure of consumers to assess properly the suitability and value of the pension products offered by the salesmen and advisers from the finance industry in turn helps to explain why they are often sold unsuitable poor-value products. In the market for most products[12] — cars, fridges, meals, travel or whatever—the relentless scrutiny and criticism of consumers ensures that those products that deliver what they promise, and which satisfy the customers who purchase them, drive out those that do not. With most products, consumers know very precisely what they want, and at what sort of price. Suppliers have to offer products that consumers want, because if they don't, they will go out of business: not enough people will purchase their products to make it profitable to produce them.

How sellers exploit buyers' ignorance

When consumers are unable or unwilling to make accurate or effective assessments of the worth of what they are buying—as is the usual case with pensions— those supplying the products have less incentive to improve them. Doing so is frequently going to be a cost without a benefit: it could prevent them from selling a product which serves their interests, because it makes them more money. As a result, the interests of the sellers of pensions get out of alignment with those who buy them. It is not in the sellers' interests to sell only products that offer the best value for money, or which suit the customers' needs best. The existence of a small number of sophisticated consumers who can assess pensions products accurately, and work out whether they provide value for money and are suitable for their particular needs, does not change that basic situation.

Xavier Gabaix and David Laibson[13] provide a model that shows very clearly why what they call 'shrouding' — the hiding of additional costs which consumers will end up paying, and which can turn the product from being good value to being a bad buy for consumers—is common in the finance industry.[14] They call those customers who, for whatever reason, don't or can't calculate the full costs of the product they are going to buy, 'myopic customers'. They conclude that: 'Firms exploit myopic customers... Nobody has an incentive to show myopic customers the error of their ways. Educating a myopic consumer... does not help the educating firm.' They note that one consequence is that 'competition will not induce firms to reveal information that would improve market efficiency'.

With pensions, it means that the finance industry will sell products whose attractiveness to customers depends on those customers' ignorance of the costs they entail.[15] It helps to explain an otherwise puzzling feature of the market in pensions: why hasn't anyone offered a low-cost pension that serves consumers better, and which forces competitors to provide products with similarly low costs? One reason is that it is inherently expensive to reach and then deal with a myriad of individual customers. For as long as providers have to pay those costs, individual pensions will remain more expensive than they could and should be. Another is that it isn't always in the interest of pension providers to provide low-cost pensions. They make money from the annual charges they take from an individual's investment account. When most customers do not seem interested in finding out exactly what those charges are, or discovering how they will erode the value of their pension investment, it is not in the interest of the providers to tell them—or to tell them in a way which is not so obscure or difficult to interpret that most of their customers either don't notice or don't care. That allows them to keep charges high, and so make more money than they would be able to, were they faced with consumers who took greater interest in their own financial futures, and were more able to work out exactly what their own financial interest consisted in.

The average consumer falls short of the rigorously rational decision-maker of economic theory in other ways. We have a tendency, to take one example, to make obvious errors when estimating probabilities.[16] But along with procrastination, the most significant bias that affects decision-making in matters that require long-term financial planning is over-optimism. We are much too willing to believe that the short-term performance of an investment is a reliable guide to the way it will perform in the long term.[17] We ignore the warnings that pension salesmen are obliged to print on their material rather in the same way that regular smokers ignore the warning 'Smoking kills' on cigarette packets. A salesman shows us that a fund manager has delivered returns of ten per cent on his investments for each of the past three years—and we leap to the conclusion that, if he were to manage our pension, he would deliver that result for the next 30 years. We don't look at the fees that will be charged. We just focus on the promised returns.

That's exactly how most pension salesmen persuade people to choose funds for their DC pensions that charge excessive fees—fees which will end up reducing the size of the customer's investment by at least 20 per cent, and sometimes much more.

Pensions and the lottery fallacy

It's perfectly legal. But it is taking advantage of the consumers' irrationality. The central irrationality is the belief that the higher returns will justify the higher fees. In the majority of cases, they won't do so. This is for the straightforward reason that the performance of most fund managers is either average or below average—so at most, the majority of them will produce returns which either don't rise above the stock market average, or actually fall below it. When you subtract their fees, the returns on an investment that they manage for the consumer will be below the stock market average.

This means that the best deal for the majority of individual pension investors cannot be to invest in a managed fund with high fees. It would be better—it would deliver higher returns—for most consumers to invest instead in a fund that simply tracks the stock market average. They charge fees that are much lower than the fees of 1.5 per cent a year or more that are common for the managed funds recommended by the pension industry. The average investor who spurns the managed funds and invests in a tracker fund will wind up with a much bigger pension—at least 20 per cent bigger— than the one who takes the advice of the finance industry and goes for managed funds.

So why does anyone follow the finance industry's advice and invest in managed funds with high fees? Ignorance of the available low-cost alternative may be part of the explanation. But over-optimism is probably more powerful: people think that they will 'win'—they believe the sales talk, and think that they have a much better chance of getting higher than average returns if they invest in a managed fund. In fact, they have a lower chance of getting such returns.

The salesmen naturally focus on the few people who actually do hit the jack pot of higher returns. This is exactly parallel to the way the advertising for the National Lottery focuses on the tiny proportion of those who buy tickets who wind up winning. The odds of winning the Lottery are too small to make it rational to buy a ticket if your aim is simply to increase your wealth. The odds of being one of those who get above-average returns, after the deduction of fees, from a managed fund over 20 or more years of investment are better than the chances of winning the Lottery—but still not good enough, given the available alternative, to make investing your savings in a managed fund with high fees a rational choice. Unless, that is, you enjoy gambling with your life savings—which most people insist they do not enjoy, and do not want to do.

We think that, as a consequence, the pensions industry's sales pitch can be seen as a variation of the 'lottery fallacy': the idea that the probability of winning the prize is enough to justify buying a ticket.

The representatives from the finance and pensions industry that we spoke to responded to this point by insisting that 'people have different attitudes to risk, and they have to be allowed to choose which risks they will take'. We agree that it is true that people have different attitudes to risk, and right that those who genuinely want to take high risks, and perhaps to gamble, with their life savings, should be allowed to. It is even true that if you enjoy gambling, then buying a lottery ticket or investing your savings in a higher-cost managed fund can be a rational thing to do. But that doesn't deal with the central point, which is that people who do not want to gamble with their savings are being encouraged, and indeed misled, into doing so by the sales pitch from the finance industry.

We don't say that salesmen and others from the pensions industry are knowingly misleading many of their customers, for judging by what those we interviewed told us, many of them are as deluded as the people they sell to: they sincerely believe that their products are 'good value'. But this does not alter the fact that most of those products are not good value for most customers, or that most of the customers who are persuaded to invest in those products are going to end up with a much smaller pension than they would have got had they ignored the advice that the 'specialists will deliver higher returns' and invested in a tracker fund instead.

Why has the finance industry served consumers so badly?

The finance industry, as a profession, has not served consumers well when it comes to personal pensions. When you go to a 'professional' for financial advice, you are entitled to expect that that advice will promote your own interests—rather than just the interests of the person giving the advice. Trust in the professional, by the consumer, is an essential part of the relationship: as a consumer, you go to a financial adviser, and listen to a pitch from a sales executive from the finance industry, because you are aware of your lack of knowledge and your tendency to make mistakes in this complicated area. You trust they will be able to get you a better deal for your investments than you would be able to for yourself. What the economists call 'informational asymmetry' is inevitable: the adviser/ financial professional knows more than you do, which of course is why you want their help. You trust that they will use the knowledge that they have—but you don't—to benefit you, rather than simply to promote their own interests to the greatest possible extent, regardless of the detrimental effect that has on you.

Very often, however, that trust in finance industry professionals has been misplaced. Some of those professionals have acted like doctors who recommend unnecessary, even dangerous, treatment, drugs or surgery solely because they benefit financially from it.[18] Any doctor who was discovered doing that would be struck off the medical register and probably prosecuted for a criminal offence. Moreover, there is a strong professional ethos among doctors, inculcated in them from the beginning of their training, of not doing anything which will harm their patients. (The first line of the Hippocratic Oath, the doctors' code, is 'First do no harm.') Although the 'informational asymmetry' inherent in the relationship between doctors and their patients—your doctor knows far more than you do about what, if anything, is wrong with you, and how to put it right—ensures that every doctor has the opportunity to harm their patients by exploiting our ignorance to recommend useless or dangerous treatments, very few ever consider it.

Why do financial advisers and salespeople from the financial sector seem so much more likely than doctors to take advantage of their customers' ignorance in order to advance their own interests? We have already suggested one reason, which is simply that they do not believe that is what they are doing: they genuinely think that their customers will benefit by following the investment strategies they recommend, even though it is clear that most of them will not.

That raises the question of why most financial advisers and salespeople do not take a more clear-sighted view of what they are in fact doing. Part of the explanation may be that, for at least the last thirty years, it has been assumed by almost everyone—economists, politicians, civil servants—helping to make policy on financial matters that if the finance industry was doing well, that must mean customers (and society more generally) were benefiting. The same people have always accepted that retail customers need more protection from financial professionals than big institutions do, and that therefore regulators should try, within reason, to protect them. But imagine you're a financial adviser who is careful to operate within the rules the regulators set. If everyone tells you that the best way you can help your customers' finances is to recommend that they do what's also best for your financial interests—by, for example, suggesting they invest in an actively managed fund that promises higher than average returns—it may be very difficult not to believe it yourself. Perhaps that's why, even after the Financial Services Authority (FSA) has placed significant restrictions on what pensions advisers and salespeople can claim and offer, many people continue to be sold products that will do more for those who sell them than they do for the people who buy them.[19]

Financial advisers and salesmen do not have a professional code equivalent to doctors' Hippocratic Oath. Would it make any difference if they did? Dan Ariely has provided some evidence that it might.[20] He and his colleagues performed a number of experiments with college students which aimed to test their honesty by providing them with opportunities to cheat. Ariely found that honesty increased if the students read the Ten Commandments first, or agreed to abide by the 'MIT Honesty Code' (it didn't matter that no such code exists: just making a public commitment to honesty was enough to improve how honestly the students in the experiments behaved).

While the results of Ariely's experiments are striking, it is not clear how much of the 'honesty effect' of making a pledge depends on the fact that in his experiments, the pledge is made only once—and the student's honesty is tested immediately afterwards. Would the effect survive if the pledge were made years before, perhaps at the beginning of an individual's career? Would it survive if instead it were repeated several times a day, before every transaction where there was an opportunity for dishonesty? Ariely doesn't explicitly consider those questions, but it is pretty clear that the answer to them is likely to be 'No'. In each case, the impact of the pledge would probably quickly fall to zero.

A basic difference between doctors and finance professionals is that the primary motivation that leads people to qualify as doctors is not usually simply to make as much money as possible. Many medical students, as well as many qualified doctors, stress that one basic reason why they chose medicine is that they are interested in science and want to help cure ill-health. That makes a significant difference to how they view their patients. There is no comparable motive in the finance industry, where the fundamental goal for most practitioners is just to make as much money as possible. Even leaving personal motivation to one side, the finance industry has a more narrowly financial incentive structure than medicine: it encourages people to focus on making as much money as possible. Were it true that the only way they could do this would be by serving consumers in the best possible way, there would be no problem. But unfortunately, it isn't true—so there is. The belief that, by promoting their own interests while remaining within regulatory rules, salespeople and financial advisers from the finance industry are bound to promote those of their customers, is false. Assuming that it must be true has contributed significantly to the very serious problem with pensions that we now face.

If financial professionals cannot be assumed, or trusted, always to do only what will be in their customers' best interests, then it is essential that those customers are well-informed enough to make their own decisions without the 'help' of financial intermediaries, or at least to be able to recognise when those intermediaries are giving them bad or self-serving advice.[21] The 'mis-selling' scandal of the 1990s forced regulators in the UK to recognise this problem. Up until very recently, the regulators have taken the view that the best way to deal with it is to ensure that consumers are provided with more, and better, information. The FSA has seen its role as being to provide 'specific education programmes to enhance knowledge and skills, thereby empowering consumers to shop around and make informed decisions which will meet their needs and personal preferences'; and also to give 'guidance to consumers... while not being prescriptive or recommending specific products and services'.[22]

The FSA certainly provided an ever-greater amount of information. But that hasn't done anything very significant to improve the quality of decision-making on financial, and in particular pension, matters by most people.[23] We're still saving too little, and investing too often in expensive pension products that promise higher returns but usually don't deliver them. The primary reason that the provision of information hasn't improved decision-making is that to make a decision, you have to process the information and use it to work out which of the available options will work best for you—and that is precisely what most people are at present unable or unwilling to do. Financial products can be very complicated: even people who work in the finance industry can be bamboozled by them. The provision of more information without the ability to process it accurately, efficiently, or indeed at all, merely leads to more confusion and procrastination.

Policy implications of the difficulty of making sensible financial decisions

At present, there are five million people in Britain contributing to a DC pension. That number is going to grow to 15 million over the next decade (see Figure 2 on p. 6).[24] All of those people are going to have to make their own decisions about how much to save, where to invest, and how much risk to take with their investments. The evidence we have surveyed suggests that many of them will make bad choices they will later regret—choices that will leave them with smaller pensions than they need and than they could have had had they chosen more skilfully.

Could financial education provide people with the skills they require to process and make rational decisions on information relating to pension products and other investments?

Those committed to the idea that the market will deliver the best results for everyone assume that the answer to that question must be 'Yes'. As Chairman of the United States Federal Reserve, Alan Greenspan was one of the leading representatives of that group. In 2005, Greenspan gave a lecture in which he noted that in the 'increasingly competitive and complex financial services market, it is essential that consumers acquire the knowledge that will enable them to evaluate products and services from competing providers and determine which best meet their long and short term needs'.[25]

Greenspan assumed that consumers could acquire the knowledge, and the skills, necessary to perform that task competently.[26] This is not a plausible belief. Lauren E. Willis surveys the available evidence and concludes that, in most cases, they can't and they won't: the gap between the level of skills people have, and the level that they would need to be able to process information on financial products sufficiently accurately to make rational decisions about which one to choose, is just too big for any financial education programme to bridge—at least any programme of financial education which people with jobs and families to look after could reasonably be expected to take.[27]

Willis also cites one study which indicates that those with a higher level of financial literacy are more likely to be victims of investment fraud than those with average levels.[28] It suggests that the source of the problem may not just be a lack of what might be called 'computational ability': the ability to do the sums needed to work out whether a particular investment product is a good deal or not. If the problem were only a lack of computational ability, then perhaps it could be solved by education. But it may be that the core difficulty lies rather with what might be called 'character traits': many people have settled dispositions—to discount the future at an excessive rate, to procrastinate over difficult decisions, to be over-optimistic about the effects of their choices— which make them intrinsically liable to make bad financial decisions. A recent FSA survey of the literature on the failures of most people to make rational decisions on matters relating to finance supported that view, concluding that, when trying to decide what to do about their own financial future, 'most people do not act as fully rational individuals who choose in their self interest... The deep-seated psychological traits at work seem fairly resistant to conventional information-based financial education and advice.'[29]

Some of those who make Government policy have reacted to that conclusion by finally deciding that it does not make much sense to continue to base pensions policy on the idea that consumers are able to maximise their own self-interest by making rational choices between the products offered to them by companies from the pensions industry.[30] They have chosen instead to follow the 'nudge' model developed by Cass Sunstein and Richard Thaler, in which employees are automatically enrolled in a low-cost DC pension scheme unless they make a conscious choice to opt out of it.[31]

This is the basis of the Government's National Employment Savings Trust [NEST], which will be discussed in Chapter 5, as will some of its problems, including the fact that, initially at least, NEST will be available only to those on low or moderate salaries. We'll investigate the implications for pension policy of recognising that, in matters of personal finance, most people do not make decisions on the model of rationality used by economic theories.

SIPPS: A case study in the effects of government policy on savers and pension providers.

Self-Invested Personal Pensions (SIPPs) have been described as 'arguably the biggest pension success story in recent years'.[32] They have certainly been a big success for the people who sell them; they can also be a good product for some people who buy them. But the issues discussed in Chapter 4 mean that some people probably lose out, too. SIPPs help to illustrate one of the flaws in the way policymakers thought about pensions for most of the last 25 years. This is the assumption that everyone is, or can be, either a confident and educated investor, or someone who can identify genuinely good-value financial advice.

Nigel Lawson introduced the Self-Invested Personal Pension (SIPP) in early 1989. Like the Personal Pension Plan (PPP), which Lawson's government had also recently introduced, the SIPP allowed individuals to manage their own pension savings outside an occupational scheme. Where it differed from the PPP was in allowing greater flexibility. A SIPP allowed the owner of the pension scheme to invest in a much wider range of investments. In the words of Standard Life's 2009 annual report (p. 302): 'A [SIPP is a] self invested personal pension which provides the policyholder with greater choice and flexibility as to the range of investments made, how those investments are managed, the administration of those assets and how retirement benefits are taken.' There was a catch: initially, the greater choice and flexibility came at the cost of higher fees.

SIPPs remained unpopular for several years after they were launched. By 1996, seven years after they had been introduced, only 7,500 had been set up. The number had still only risen to 90,000 by 2003.[33] To put this in context, by then almost 11 million people had taken out either a PPP or a stakeholder pension.[34]

But a raft of new pension legislation that came into force on 6 April 2006 (known as 'A-Day' within the pensions industry) made SIPPs more attractive. For example, it allowed someone to set up a SIPP *in addition* to any occupational scheme to which they already belonged, and so receive the tax benefits of saving for a pension in two separate arrangements.

Financial intermediaries proceeded to exploit this new opportunity with their usual vigour.[35] 'Arguably the biggest pension success story in recent years,' begins a 2010 marketing brochure from one firm, 'has been the rise of the SIPP (Self Invested Personal Pension).'[36] One of the biggest beneficiaries was a company founded in only 1995 called AJ Bell.[37] Its profits of less than £1 million in 2003 had grown to more than £16 million in 2010, mostly from the SIPP business. Here is how the company described itself in its 2007 annual report:

> Our vision has helped shape the SIPP market. Until the launch of Sippdeal, the UK's first online SIPP, SIPPs were viewed as a niche product suitable only for high net worth individuals. How that has changed in the last seven years! We recognised and subsequently helped drive the polarisation of the SIPP market into three distinct sectors. The traditional bespoke market, the low-cost online direct-to-consumer market and the low-cost funds-based adviser-led market. We are the only SIPP provider that successfully delivers SIPPs into each of these markets.[38]

The first three products mentioned on page 7 of the company's 2010 annual report are **Sippcentre, Sippdeal** and **Sippdealxtra.** And that's not to mention another of 2010's innovations: '**SippTalk.tv**, our new online video channel for advisers and clients'.

By the end of 2009, with the help of organisations such as AJ Bell, 500,000 people had set up a SIPP.[39] The number had grown by a factor of five in the course of just six years. Over the same period, the number of Personal Pension Plans fell by one fifth and Stakeholder Pensions stagnated.[40]

Not surprisingly, this kind of growth began to attract attention from the media and from regulators. It raised alarming echoes of the rush into Personal Pension Plans that had taken place almost exactly twenty years before. On 28 May 2008, Reuters ran a story called 'SIPPs: sexy pensions or the next mis-selling scandal?' In November 2008 Malcolm McLean, the Pensions Regulator, warned of the 'very real prospect of another mis-selling scandal' in SIPPs.[41] The following month the Financial Services Authority (FSA) published a formal review of the area, observing that: 'Switching into personal pensions and SIPPs from existing arrangements can be an appropriate move for many people, but this is a complex area of business where consumers rely heavily upon advisers.'[42]

What was really going on here? The SIPP success story has two sides. For some buyers, the new generation SIPP really is an attractive and appropriate product. As AJ Bell noted, costs have come down, making the product available to a wider market. The 'greater choice and flexibility' that Standard Life mentioned is real: at least one SIPP provider offers more than 2,000 possible investments, far more than would be available under one of the old Personal Pension Plans.[43] And improved information technology brings convenience as well. As one firm explains in its SIPP brochure: 'An additional benefit of transferring your existing pensions into a SIPP means [sic] you can see your entire pension provision in one place. This can help you and your Broker to choose investments as you can easily see all current investments in one statement.'[44]

If you are a confident investor who wants to take control, then the reduced (though not necessarily low) costs, wide choice and convenience of a new SIPP make it a very suitable and attractive product. For the last 25 years, policymakers have implicitly assumed that everyone is, or can become, like you. Using that assumption, SIPPs are a valuable innovation by the market. The profits intermediaries have made from selling them are a sign that the world has become a better (more efficient) place. For some people, as already noted, that is probably true.

Unfortunately, as we discussed in Chapter 4, not everyone is, or will soon become, a confident or educated investor. Changes in the pension system are creating millions of 'accidental investors' and we suspect that only a small minority of them could be described as confident or educated. But they are all potential SIPP buyers, whether a SIPP is suitable for them or not.

A few financial intermediaries continue to be caught selling individual pensions in a way that formally breaks the rules. The fact that rules get broken is hardly a secret. 'There's a bandwagon effect going on,' Malcolm Cuthbert, managing director of financial planning at independent financial services firm Killik & Co, told Reuters in May 2008. 'In the same way that people got into the tech boom, they're now getting into SIPPs, and sometimes individuals are going from a life company personal pension to a life company hybrid SIPP, and are paying more for effectively the same investments. There's quite a lot of that going on.'[45]

The FSA's December 2008 review of pension switching,[46] found that one sixth of the 500 cases it looked at had involved 'unsuitable advice'. The FSA noted specifically:

The main reasons we considered the advice to be unsuitable were:

- the switch involved extra product costs without good reason (79 per cent of unsuitable cases);

- the fund(s) recommended were not suitable for the customer's attitude to risk and personal circumstances (40 per cent of unsuitable cases);

- the adviser failed to explain the need for, or put in place, ongoing reviews when these are necessary (26 per cent of unsuitable cases); and

- the switch involved loss of benefits from the ceding scheme without good reason (14 per cent of unsuitable cases).[47]

The FSA wrote to all of the 4,500 firms involved in advising on pension switches, reminding them of their obligations, and mentioned that some of the firms it had investigated would be facing 'enforcement action'.[48] Indeed, between November 2008 and 16 February 2011 the FSA seems to have taken formal action against at least seven firms involved in pension switching.[49] One of these cases provides some anecdotal colour on how rules are broken in the pension transfer market.

On 10 November 2008 the FSA issued a Penalty Notice against a firm of financial advisers called AWD Chase de Vere Wealth Management Limited.[50] AWD Chase de Vere was fined for business it had carried out between 28 February 2006 and 31 October 2007—in other words, precisely the period when 'A-Day' (6 April 2006) suddenly made SIPPs more attractive. At the time, it employed 280 advisers in a number of branches around the UK. The firm was the result of combining several smaller ones. Its immediate parent in the UK, AWD Group plc, was owned at the time by a Germany company called AWD Holdings AG.[51]

During the roughly one-and-a-half years in question, AWD Chase de Vere advisers sold a total of 4,300 pension switches to 2,800 customers. This generated about £8.6

million of revenue (fees) for the firm. To put this in context, its parent AWD Group reported sales of about £165 million for the full two years ending December 2008, which means pension switches as a whole represented five per cent or more of AWD Chase de Vere's total sales over that period.

The FSA found that almost one-third of these pension-related deals involved unsuitable advice (1,200 of the 4,300 transactions, involving 829 out of the 2,800 total customers involved). It fined AWD Chase de Vere £1.6 million, or about one fifth of all the pension-related revenue. With the benefit of a standard 30 per cent discount for prompt payment, AWD Chase de Vere paid £1.12 million and also agreed to compensate the customers involved. Net of insurance cover, the compensation seems to have cost it a further £1.3 million over the next couple of years.

AWD Chase de Vere was not the only company to be served with an enforcement notice by the FSA on this issue.[52] The FSA complimented the firm for the way it moved to improve its practices after being fined:[53] there have been major personnel changes at all levels of the firm and it has done well in several industry surveys.

All credit to the FSA for catching and fining AWD Chase de Vere and the other firms. It has shown a determination not to be caught out in the way the FSA's predecessors were by the personal pension mis-selling scandal of 1988-94. Levying fines on misbehaving firms sends a clear message to others, though since there's no way of proving a negative it's impossible to tell how much illegal behaviour the FSA's actions have prevented.

It is unclear how many of the improper pension switches that the FSA identified across the industry involved SIPPs in particular. For example, some might have involved switching between a Stakeholder Pension and a Personal Pension Plan. So it could be argued that the FSA actions do not suggest anything particularly negative about the SIPP.

But selling a SIPP does not have to be illegal, or break any FSA rules, in order to be inappropriate. As one spokesman from within the industry pointed out recently: 'A number of personal pensions now have a more than adequate range of fund options and there is little point in paying for added bells and whistles if they're not needed.'[54] A SIPP is suitable for a confident investor who wants to take control. How many people are like that? We believe that description fits only a minority of the 'accidental investors' created by changes in the UK's pensions systems.

Most people are more like this: 'If you do not want to think about your pension or move your money around and simply want to invest a regular amount and forget about it, then a SIPP is not for you.'

We think this second description nicely captures most of the 'accidental investors' that the UK's pension changes have created. The DB pension schemes that they used to belong to satisfied their needs. In the final chapter we urge policymakers to find ways to re-create at least some of that kind of framework for most pension consumers.

In the absence of that kind of framework, we believe there is a danger that 'accidental investors' will be tempted or persuaded to buy products like SIPPs even though they are not really 'confident and educated investors'. This will be neither illegal, nor even detectible by a regulator such as the FSA.

Why do we think this? Because incentives matter; selling SIPPs is profitable; and the finance industry contains its share of good salesmen. 'The defining criterion... is how much interest you want to take in your pension,' one representative told the *Daily Telegraph* in a 2008 article about SIPPs. 'If you do not want to think about your pension or move your money around and simply want to invest a regular amount and forget about it, then a Sipp is not for you. However, if you want to take an interest in your money then a Sipp may be the best option. It does not matter if you do not know what to invest in; you can ask an investment adviser to make the decisions for you.'[55]

As already suggested, the first two sentences describe how most people feel about their pensions. 'Simply want to invest a regular amount and forget about it' describes the way things used to be in the world of defined benefit (DB) pensions. But that world is vanishing fast. Consumers are anxious about their uncertain financial futures and changes in UK pensions have left many of them without any simple alternative. It probably isn't too hard for intermediaries to persuade them that they ought to 'take an interest in [their] money'. After all, how could you *not* 'take an interest in your money'? From there it is just a short step to 'ask an investment adviser to make the decisions for you'.

It would be foolish to expect financial intermediaries not to try to sell their products. The FSA deserves credit for doing a better job of enforcement and deterrence with SIPPs than its predecessors did twenty years ago when personal pensions were introduced. But even if regulators catch everyone who breaks the rules, can we be confident that most people end up with the right product? In a market where the product is always going to be too complex for most consumers to understand, we don't see how anyone can be.

500,000 people have now set up a SIPP. Is it plausible that all of them genuinely value and/or use the extra flexibility that a SIPP provides? We doubt it. We think that what many of these SIPP holders would really like to do is (broadly, not literally) 'invest a regular amount and forget about it'. Is a SIPP right for you if that's all you want to do? The short answer is No. In Chapter 5 we look at how policymakers could take better account of the needs of 'accidental investors'.

5

What Next?

My fear is that society will go through a whole generation without DB plans before we discover that current DC arrangements typically do not provide an adequate post-retirement income.

Don Ezra[1]

Our analysis of what has gone wrong with pension provision in Britain over the last 25 years raises a number of basic questions. The most fundamental is the extent to which it makes sense to try to increase individuals' responsibility for saving for, and managing, their own pensions.

Let us be clear: individuals must and should always have a degree of personal responsibility for their own financial futures. Taking it away altogether would obviously be tyrannical, coercive and unjust, as well as chronically economically inefficient and ultimately unsustainable. So the issue is not whether individuals should be given any responsibility at all for their own pensions. The issue rather is *how much* responsibility public policy should aim to give to individuals for creating and managing their own pensions.

Policy in Britain has been devoted to increasing individual responsibility to an ever-greater extent. Behind that lies the idea that individual people, acting in their own self-interest within the framework of a competitive market, will produce the best possible results for everyone. The same idea lay behind the decision by policy-makers to adopt a framework of 'light touch' regulation for the whole financial sector. The financial crisis of 2008, when many of Britain and America's biggest banks and finance houses would have gone bankrupt had they not been bailed out with money from taxpayers, has led to an agonised reappraisal of how far that idea can or should be applied to the financial sector.[2]

We think the impact that the same idea has had on individual pensions means that its application should be reappraised here as well.

The crisis of 2008 was the result of decisions taken by financial experts: people working for the banks who lived and breathed financial data. If anyone is capable of handling complicated financial issues, these people were. But policymakers had let them play by a set of rules that encouraged them to take far too many risks; and many of them fell victim to some of the same syndromes that distort decision-making by the rest of us—chronic over-optimism being the most obvious. If even these people turn out to be incapable of acting rationally[3] when taking financial decisions, it makes it much harder to believe that everyone else should be.

Many of the pension products offered to ordinary consumers have now become so complicated, with so many different fees and charges, that even were most people not subject to the biases and irrationalities outlined in the last chapter, it is increasingly implausible to maintain that we are all able to assess them accurately, rank them, and then choose the best option. To make the right decision, most of us are bound to be dependent on advice. The trouble is, we cannot rely on the advice that pension salesmen and advisers give: too often, following it has proved to be not in the best interests of the consumers who receive it.

The explanation for that situation is not that pension salesmen or financial advisers are inherently bad people, or don't want to do the best for their clients. It is rather that, like most people, they do want to do the best for themselves. The combination of the financial incentives that govern what they can do, together with the policy decision to make individual consumers responsible for managing their own pensions, make it unlikely that the result will be that consumers end up with pensions that will suit their needs.

Public policy on pensions needs to be framed around recognising that most individuals are not willing or able to take the decisions they need to if they are to wind up with decent pensions; and that following the advice of salesmen and financial advisers won't usually solve that problem.

One way to end those difficulties would be to take the decision totally out of the hands of individuals, and give it to state bureaucrats: pensions would be 'collectivised', and any individual responsibility for pension provision would be eliminated. As will be obvious, we don't think this would be a sensible way to proceed. It would require the use of state coercion to an unacceptable degree, not least because it would deprive people of the opportunity to manage their own pensions. We do not think anyone should be deprived of that opportunity: anyone who believes they will do better by actively managing their own pension fund should be allowed to do so. But it should not be the aim of state policy on pensions to push everyone into that position. Most people don't want to do it, aren't equipped to do it, and will make choices they will regret if they are forced to do it. So we think that pensions policy should aim to make it easy for people to save regularly throughout their working lives as members of large funds which they can trust to look after their interests.

We recognise that is essential to ensure that there is at least some link between what an individual saves for their pension and what they receive in their retirement. That link can be preserved while diminishing the extent to which individuals are required, or encouraged, either by law or by regulations, to create and manage their own pension. In the past, pension policy has concentrated on making people responsible for creating their own individual pension plans and forced them to become amateur asset managers. But wholly individual plans have turned out to be an inefficient and expensive way of providing pensions. Most individuals do much better on average if they belong to a large DC scheme, for example, than if they arrange an individual private pension for themselves: charges are lower, and there will be less pressure to gamble funds.

To see the benefits of belonging to a large scheme, just consider Colin from Chapter 2. He has a defined contribution (DC) scheme that lacks the benefits of scale. We showed in Chapter 2 how high charges, and stopping and starting, take their toll.

Now compare Colin with his older sister Sally. She belongs to a large DC pension scheme provided by her employer. Sally's employer buys fund management in bulk, so it can pass on much lower charges to Sally. Remember: by reducing your charges by just one per cent a year, you can improve your retirement income by 25 per cent. Sally is also much less likely to stop and start her saving, because her employer provides a sensible set of 'default' fund options so that she will not be under constant pressure to decide whether she should switch her pension to the latest 'high returns' fund. In taking an active interest in his own pension, Colin will try to chase the highest returns he can find. That will mean he is likely to switch his pension to the fund where returns are highest—at least for this quarter.

The benefits of not being on your own

About five million private sector employees are currently saving in DC pension schemes. Some, like Sally, benefit from economies of scale and a helpful employer. Others, like Colin, do not. Still others may have decided that they want to take full control, completely on their own, with a product like the SIPPs we discussed in Chapter 4. Over the next decade, this group overall is expected to grow by ten million.[4] We think that government policy should aim to enable and encourage as many as possible of those people to join large schemes provided by employers which offer very low charges, which do not require individuals to actively manage their own funds, and where the employer contributes to the employees' pension savings.

The creation of the National Employment Savings Trust (NEST), which is due to come into operation in 2012, is a significant step in the right direction. A version of NEST was recommended by the 2002 Pensions Commission headed by Adair Turner, and it has been adopted by the present Government. Every company will be required to provide a qualifying pension scheme. No company will have to join NEST—but if a company does, NEST will offer benefits both to the company and to its employees.

If an employer joins NEST, NEST will automatically enrol qualifying employees onto a company pension scheme. It will be open to every employee to decide to opt out. But the 'default' position—that is, what will happen if you don't make any decision—is that you will be enrolled.

This should lead to a very large diminution in the 50 per cent of employees in the private sector who are not saving for retirement *at all*. The Department of Work and Pensions thinks that, once NEST is in place, between three and six million people who are not currently saving for a pension will start doing so.[5] Qualifying employees will be those earning £5,035-33,540 (levels to be reviewed annually), and their annual contributions will be capped at £4,200 (for the 2011/2012 tax year). Employees will contribute four per cent of their annual earnings. Employers will add a further three per cent. The government will then contribute an additional one per cent, which means that each employee will save a total of eight per cent of their salary. NEST will manage the pension pots. Its annual management charge will be very low: a mere 0.3 per cent per annum, although each contribution will attract a one-time 'contribution charge' of 1.8 per cent. Still, the Pensions Commission estimated that this level of saving over a working life, combined with low charges, would increase the retirement income of a [median] earner from about 30 per cent of their working level to about 45 per cent. That means millions of people will be 50 per cent better off in retirement.

There are problems with NEST. One is the IT system that will be used for running it. No one has yet identified a computer system that will be able to handle the millions of pension accounts in a sufficiently reliable way. The Japanese computer system rendered 50 million pensions accounts unusable after a glitch in 1997.[6] It should not be impossible to develop a sufficiently reliable and effective computer system that can handle the data properly. But so far, the British government's experience with IT systems has not been a happy one: the NHS computerisation of medical records has so far cost £12 billion, and still doesn't work as intended. It does not bode well for the purchase of NEST's computer system.

But the most serious problem with NEST is not the technical problem of purchasing reliable computers. It is the decision to limit contributions that any individual can make to it to (initially) £4,200 a year. The effect will be to deter several million people who would otherwise be able to benefit from NEST's lower charges. They won't be able to do so, at least until the cap is removed. A recent review of NEST recommended that the cap should be removed in 2017.[7] We will have to wait and see whether that recommendation is turned into policy.

Why has the cap on contributions been introduced? There appear to be two reasons. One is to save the Treasury money. Contributions to NEST, as pension savings, are tax free. If large numbers of people currently not saving start contributing to NEST every year, the Treasury stands to lose a significant amount of tax revenue. The Government has not stated in public that the potential loss of revenue explains why it has adopted the cap—no doubt because they are aware that telling that millions of people they are to be deprived of the opportunity to invest in low-cost pensions because the Treasury would lose money would not go down well with the electorate.

But at least that rationale has some logic to it. The other reason for the cap has no publicly justifiable basis to it at all: the authors have been told that the cap was imposed in order to placate the pensions industry, which complained that it would face 'unfair' competition. It is true that pensions providers would face competition from

NEST's low charges—but although that may not be in the interests of the industry, it *is* in the interest of consumers: it would help to lower the often excessively high charges currently levied by firms offering individual pension funds. It would, that is, bring about the outcome that competition between pension providers was meant to— but signally failed to achieve.

We think that NEST should be extended to the widest possible extent, and any cap on individual contributions removed. Using the work-place is the quickest and most obvious way to provide people with larger schemes. Generally, people trust their employers to provide fair pensions more than they trust salesmen and advisers from the finance industry. And generally, they are right to do so. Employers communicate regularly with their employees, and they pay them—two features of the relationship which help to reduce the costs of pension provision.

The costs of greater choice

The pensions industry will object that NEST will diminish consumer choice. But at present, the amount of choice available in pension investments does not actually help consumers get the best for their money. The basic reason for this is that consumers, as we have emphasised, are not in a position to assess and rank the options available to them. Most of us don't know which of the myriad of options available is the best one for us, and most of us can't work it out. The vast range of choices available don't help us get low-cost pensions. In fact, the range of choices *adds* costs.

The 'price' you pay for a pension investment fund essentially consists in the charges of around 1.5 per cent a year that you agree to pay when you sign up for it. The cost of 'producing' that fund—the cost to the pension company of paying the people who decide what your pension will be invested in—may be as low as 0.1 per cent.[8] The fund manager and his company don't simply pocket the difference. He or his firm has to pay a great deal for advertising and marketing in order to persuade consumers to purchase *this* product rather than one from his many competitors: the lion's share of the 1.5 per cent charges goes to paying for marketing.

That helps to explain why, in the pensions industry, increasing consumer choice has increased costs to the consumer without producing any significant benefits. If the array of choice had brought down costs very significantly; if it had provided products that enabled consumers to choose precisely the option that would work best for them; then the vast array of choices available in pension investments would be 'worth it' to consumers. But because it does not have those consequences, we do not think the claim that pension policies which make it easy for consumers to join large, low-cost funds would 'diminish the number of investment choices' is much of a count against them.

We think that the industry would serve consumers better if it confronted consumers with fewer choices. Indeed, we think policy makers should aim for a market structure which features a small number of very large pension providers. The large providers would have much less need to spend large sums on advertising, marketing and distribution. They would be able to pass on to their customers the resulting savings. And that should mean that the average cost to consumers of buying a pension comes sharply down.

The benefits of a return to sharing risks

Policy-makers should also explore ways in which pension schemes can retrieve some of the collective benefits of risk-sharing that have been progressively abandoned over the last 25 years. Few people would say it was a good idea for anyone to arrange their own health insurance on an individual basis: the benefits from doing it as part of a large group are just too great. Pensions provide an opportunity for sharing not just one, but two forms of risk: investment risk (while the pension pot is being built up) and longevity risk (life in retirement). And yet over the last 25 years, government policies have led to our progressively turning our backs on the collective benefit of sharing these risks. The costs, as we saw in Chapter 2, will be huge.

Chapter 3 showed how this happened. Politicians favoured private, individual pensions because they thought it was a way to make pensions affordable. But it wasn't. Meanwhile, legal and accounting changes that were designed to save defined benefit (DB) pensions actually succeeded in killing them off.

We believe both these factors were the direct or indirect result of an over-simplistic conviction that, if left as far as possible to themselves, free markets would deliver better results for everyone. That embrace of the ideology of the market has now lasted for more than a generation. There is evidence to suggest that, spurred on by the crash of 2008, politicians and other policymakers are starting to realise that free markets can create, as well as solve, economic problems. But as yet, that realisation has yet to result in any significant policy changes.

How can policy-makers encourage individuals saving for pensions to become members of larger schemes that enable them to share risks? The first step is to recognise that a pension scheme does not have to be *either* DB *or* DC. It can combine elements of both: there is a continuous spectrum from one extreme to the other. Figure 8 illustrates this in schematic form:

Figure 8: Schematic illustration of Defined Benefit vs. Defined Contribution

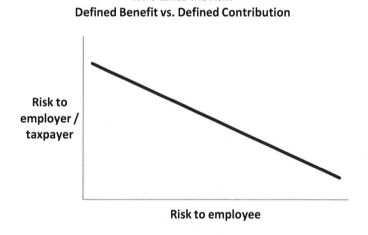

Who takes the risk?
Defined Benefit vs. Defined Contribution

Risk to employer / taxpayer

Risk to employee

Source: after Johnson, 'Self-sufficiency is the Key'

Old-style defined benefit (DB) schemes occupy the top 'northwest' corner: up there, employers (or taxpayers, in the case of public sector pension schemes) take on all the risks and headaches. Over the last 25 years, millions of private sector employees have skidded vertiginously, and largely unconsciously, to the bottom 'southeast' corner. Here they have defined contribution (DC) pension plans that are not really pensions at all, and will provide much lower retirement incomes.

Public sector employees, who mostly still have defined benefit (DB) plans, remain in Figure 8's 'northwest'. This creates a huge gap between the public and private sectors, which is going to cause an increasing amount of political and economic stress. Every government in the foreseeable future will likely be looking for ways to move public sector employees 'southeast' as well.[9]

But there is a middle ground between DB (as it used to be) and DC. One way of finding pensions that occupy that middle ground, and which combine elements of both DC and DB, is to loosen the pension promise involved in a DB scheme. One reason why many employers wanted to discontinue their DB schemes was that 1995's Goode Report tightened a best-efforts pension promise into a contractual guarantee. Clearly, from an employee's point of view, a best-efforts promise is not as good as a contractual guarantee. But it is better than no promise at all, which is where most people have ended up. In effect, the Goode Report's well-meaning attempt to create the best (a contractual guarantee) drove out the good (a best-efforts promise). Introducing 'safety valves' into a DB promise might make a revised form of DB plan feasible again for employers. For example, inflation protection could be loosened, and retirement age could be linked to life expectancy.[10] Employees would have to share some of the risk with employers—but this would still be likely to leave them better off than they are in a DC plan.[11]

****

This report has shown how easy it is to get public policy on pensions wrong. Most of the policy initiatives relating to pensions over the past 25 years have made the situation worse: their overall effect has been to reduce the post-retirement income that most people are going to receive. No-one in Parliament, from the pensions industry, or framing regulations intended to produce that result, any more than the millions of people working, getting older, and worrying about their financial future intended it. But it is what has happened.

The first step to doing something about it is to recognise how badly things have gone wrong. This report should have persuaded its readers to take that first step.

As we have emphasised, the tendency to put off difficult decisions is very common. Procrastination has bad enough effects on its own. But when it is linked with over-optimism, as it frequently is, the result is extremely damaging. Critical decisions are not taken, and the inaction gets justified on the basis that it's better that way: things will work out and 'right themselves'.

With pensions, they certainly will not. Ten million people alive today are going to live to be a hundred. Unless effective action is taken to increase the amount people save, and the effectiveness with which those savings are converted into post-retirement income, poverty amongst older people is going to increase on an enormous scale.

References

Ambachtseer, Keith, *Pension Revolution*, New York: Wiley, 2007.

Ariely, Dan, *Predictably Irrational: the Hidden Forces that Shape our Decisions*, London: Harpercollins, 2009.

Blake, David, 'Two decades of pension reform in the UK: what are the implications for occupational pensions?' Pensions Institute, Cass Business School, March 2000.

Blake, David, Byrne, Alistair, Harrison, Debbie and Rhodes, Bill, 'Pyrrhic victory? The unintended consequences of the Pensions Act 2004', Cass Business School and the Pensions Institute, 2005.

Booth, Philip, 'Britain's pension problem: government failure', *Freeman*, May 2005, vol.5, issue 4.

Booth, Philip and Cooper, D., *The Way out of the Pension Quagmire*, Institute of Economic Affairs, 2005.

Boeri, Tito, Bovenberg, Lans, Coeure, Benoit and Roberts, Andrew, 'Dealing with the new giants: rethinking the role of pension funds', Geneva Reports on the World Economy 8, CEPR, 2006.

Congdon, Tim, 'The pension commission: is Adair Turner irrational or confused?' *Economic Affairs*, March 2005.

De Meza, David, Irlenbusch, Bernd and Reyniers, Diane, 'Financial capability: a behavioural economics perspective', Financial Services Authority, 2008.

Dennett, Laurie, *A Sense of Security: 150 years of the Prudential*, Granta, 1998.

Department for Work and Pensions, 'Review of international pension reform', 2010.

The Economist, 'The end of the company pension', 15 May 1999.

Ellis, Charles, 'Where were we?', *Financial Analysts Journal,* Vol. 63 No. 1, 2007.

Ezra, Don, 'Defined-benefit and defined-contribution plans of the future', *Financial Analysts Journal,* Vol. 63, No. 1, 2007.

Financial Services Authority, 'Quality of advice on pension switching—a report on the findings of a thematic review', December 2008.

Fowler, Norman, *Ministers Decide: A Personal Memoir of the Thatcher Years*, London: Chapman's, 1991.

Gabaix, Xavier and Laibson, David, 'Shrouded attributes, consumer myopia, and information suppression in competitive markets', MIT Dept of Economics Working Paper 05-18.

Goode, Roy, 'Pension Law Reform—the report of the Pension Law Review Committee', HMSO, 1993.

Government Actuary's Department, "Occupational pension schemes 2000', April 2003, available at

REFERENCES

http://www.statistics.gov.uk/downloads/theme_social/Oc
c_Pension/OPSS_Pension_Scheme_2000.pdf

Greenspan, Alan, 'Consumer Finance', lecture at the
Federal Reserve System's Fourth Annual Community
Affairs Research Conference, Washington, DC, 8 April
2005.

Hancock, Ruth, *et al.*, 'Projections of owner-occupation
rates, house values, income and financial assets among
older people, UK, 2002-2022', Personal Social Services
Research Unit, Discussion Paper 2373.

Hastings, Max, 'Forget financial advisers: I wish I'd
stuffed my cash into the mattress', *Guardian*, 2 March
2009.

HM Treasury, 'The UK pension annuities market:
structure, trends & innovation', January 2009.

Hutton, John, Independent Public Service Pensions
Commission: Final Report, March 2011, http://cdn.hm-
treasury.gov.uk/hutton_final_100311.pdf

Johnson, Michael, 'Simplification is the key', Centre for
Policy Studies, London, June 2010; 'Self-sufficiency is the
key', Centre for Policy Studies, London: February 2011.

Johnson, Paul, Yeandle, David and Boulding, Adrian,
'Making automatic enrolment work', DWP, October 2010.

Keating, Con, 'Don't stop thinking about tomorrow', *Long
Finance*, 2010.

113

Lawson, Nigel, *The View from Number 11*, London, 1992.

McLean, Malcolm, 'Credit crunch pressure may wrongly encourage projected rights transfers into SIPPs', Occupational Pensions Defence Union, November 2008.

Millar, Frederick and Rogers, Frederick, *Old Age Pensions—Pros and Cons*, London: Isbister, 1903.

Murthi, Mamta, Orszag, J. Michael and Orszag, Peter R., 'Administrative Costs under a Decentralized Approach to Individual Accounts: Lessons from the United Kingdom', World Bank, 2001.

Nozick, Robert, *Anarchy, State and Utopia*, New York, 1974.

Odean, Terrance, 'Volume, volatility, price and profit when all traders are above average', *The Journal of Finance*, Vol. 53, No. 6, Dec, 1998, pp. 1887-1934.

Office for National Statistics, 'Occupational Pension Schemes Annual Report', 2009; *Social Trends 40* (2010); Pension Trends; http://www.statistics.gov.uk/pensiontrends/

Organisation for Economic Cooperation and Development, 'Pensions at a glance 2009: retirement-income systems in OECD countries'.

Pension Protection Fund, 'PPF 7800 Index'; available at http://www.pensionprotectionfund.org.uk/Pages/PPF7800 Index.aspx

REFERENCES

Pensions Commission, *Turner Report*, 2005.

Pensions Policy Institute, 'Retirement income and assets: outlook for the future', July 2010; 'Pensions Primer', May 2010; 'A Foundation Pension', June 2010; 'Pension Facts', October 2010.

Pitt-Watson, David, 'Pensions for the people: addressing the savings and investment crisis in Britain', RSA, 2009; 'Tomorrow's investor: building the consensus for a people's pension in Britain', RSA 2010.

Rhodes, Gerald, *Public Sector Pensions*, George Allen and Unwin, 1965.

Samuelson, Paul, 'An exact consumption-loan model of interest with or without the social contrivance of money', *Journal of Political Economy*, December 1958.

Siegel, Laurence and Barton Waring, M., 'Don't kill the golden goose! Saving pension plans', *Financial Analysts Journal*, Vol. 63, No. 1, February 2007.

Stiglitz, Joseph, *Freefall*, New York: Norton, 2010.

Sunstein, Cass R. and Thaler, Richard H., 'Liberal paternalism is not an oxymoron', May 2003; http://www.law.uchicago.edu/Lawecon/index.html

Sunstein, Cass R. and Thaler, Richard H., *Nudge: Improving Decisions About Health, Wealth and Happiness*, Yale, 2008.

Turner, Adair, 'Reforming finance: are we being radical enough?', Clare Distinguished Lecture in Economics and Public Policy, February 18, 2011.

Thatcher, Margaret, Interview with *Woman's Own*, 31 October, 1987. Full transcript available at http://www.margaretthatcher.org/document/106689

Whitehouse, Edward, 'Pension reform, financial literacy and public information: a case study of the United Kingdom', World Bank, January 2000.

Willis, Lauren, 'Against financial-literacy education', *Iowa Law Review*, 2008.

Notes

Introduction

1   We acknowledge our debt to Ellis (2007) for this approach.

2   Organisation for Economic Cooperation and Development, 'Pensions at a Glance, 2009—Retirement-Income Systems in OECD countries', p. 98.

1: How Pensions Get Paid For

1   That group includes politicians. Before the 2010 election, David Cameron was asked how much the state pension paid people entitled to it every week. He got the answer wrong.

2   This is denied by some analysts, who claim that any shortfall can be made up by the Government, ultimately by the expedient of printing more money.

3   It has some: for instance, loans from organisations such as the IMF or from other countries. But of course, those organisations are only willing to extend loans to a state that has a stable and reliable tax base, which can only come from taxes on individual people and their companies.

4   This deliberately extreme illustration assumes that both pension pots were invested entirely in the UK stock market and ignores any changes in annuity rates between October 2007 and March 2009.

5   In an article for *Newsweek* in 1967. The academic paper he wrote on the topic is 'An Exact Consumption-Loan Model of Interest with or without the Social Contrivance of Money', *The Journal of Political Economy*, Volume LXVI December 1958 Number 6.

6   Robert Rowthorn, Emeritus Professor of Economics at Cambridge, pointed out to us that Samuelson over-stated this point. 'Unfunded PAYG schemes are not intrinsically

Ponzi schemes. They are only Ponzi schemes if they promise benefits that are predicated on unrealistic expectations about future productivity grown.' [R. Rowthorn, private communication.] The difficulty is in identifying when the promised benefits are based on 'unrealistic expectations'.

7 This is the theme of dozens of papers warning of a funding catastrophe ahead for pensions in the UK. Michael Johnson's paper for the Centre for Policy Studies is one of the most recent and most persuasive: 'Self-sufficiency is the key' (February 2011). Johnson says that 'public sector pensions are unfair and funded in the style of Madoff', and that their financing will soon collapse 'under the weight of insufficient contributions, rising longevity, and an aging workforce'.

8 DB pension schemes vary, making it difficult to generalise. A 'healthy percentage' usually means between one-half and two-thirds. Final, rather than career average salary, used to be the most common base. This created a structural bias in favour of high earners, but most people believe this was just practical as opposed to a conspiracy: before computers, it was easier to keep track of a final salary than of a career average.

9 We have been unable to track down DB contribution levels that prevailed in the 1970s, but it is safe to say they were lower than they are now. As recently as 2000, the average DB pension contribution was 16.2% of salary (5.0% employee, 11.2% employer)—Government Actuary's Department, 'Occupational pension schemes 2000'. Table 1 shows that today's figure is 21.6% (4.9% employee, 16.6% employer).

2: Why Are Defined Contribution (DC) Pensions Such a Bad Deal?

1 Gerald Rhodes, *Public Sector Pensions*, George Allen and Unwin, 1965.

2   In 1980, annuity rates were 16 per cent, meaning a £100,000
    pension pot would buy an income of £16,000. Just over ten
    years ago they were 10 per cent (income: £10,000). Today
    they are at all-time lows of around six per cent (income:
    £6,000). Source: HM Treasury, 'The UK Pension Annuities
    Market: Structure, Trends & Innovation', January 2009;
    available at http://cis.ier.hit-
    u.ac.jp/Japanese/society/conference0901/lewis-paper.pdf ;
    press reports. Note that annuity rates depend on the
    features included (e.g. single or dual life, flat rate or
    inflation-protected). Precise comparisons over time would
    require consistent data series, which do not seem to be
    available. The first two figures here come from a HM
    Treasury document which does not specify the precise terms
    of the annuity involved. We believe the figures give a good
    sense of the order of magnitude and direction of travel.

3   As Laurence Siegel and M. Barton Waring (*Financial Analysts
    Journal*, 2007) put it: 'Taking all these factors into
    consideration, it's clear that few employees can ever expect a
    secure and prosperous retirement with reasonable income
    replacement from a DC-plan structure alone; for most, it is,
    at best, a very small contributor to retirement income. It is
    small enough that we are kidding ourselves when we even
    speak the phrase "defined-contribution retirement plan".
    As they are typically configured today, they aren't
    retirement plans at all, but modest savings plans. They
    might supplement a DB plan or other retirement income in
    small ways, but they aren't replacements for them.'

4   Michael Johnson's report 'Self-sufficiency is the Key' (Centre
    for Policy Studies, February 2011) discusses the difference
    between public and private sector pensions in some detail.

5   This is for illustrative purposes. In practice, very few
    companies like this still exist.

6   This is a generic description of what might take the legal form of a 'Group Personal Pension' or 'Group Stakeholder Pension' or 'Group SIPP'.

7   *The Economist*, 'The End of the Company Pension', 15 May 1999. To be fair, the DC scheme that a large company like Sainsbury's was offering may have featured lower fees than Colin's. But it is still shocking to see a large company actively trying to persuade employees to switch from DB to DC (and encouraging to see that so many of them apparently knew better).

8   Note one small simplification. Brian personally contributed about five per cent of his salary every year, while Colin contributed about three per cent. In principle, Colin had a choice between spending the extra two per cent each year or adding it to his savings. Ignoring tax benefits, the latter would have increased his overall annual pension contribution from 41 per cent of Brian's level to 50 per cent (i.e. 11 divided by 22).

9   Both the framework and the figures for the next three points are derived from Mamta Murthi, J. Michael Orszag, and Peter R. Orszag, 'Administrative Costs under a Decentralized Approach to Individual Accounts: Lessons from the United Kingdom', World Bank, 2001. We are not aware of any more recent update of this work using current figures. The framework would still apply in any case, and we believe the figures would not change substantially (the authors made a point of being conservative, i.e. cautious, in the figures they eventually used).

10 1.5 per cent is also where annual charges on Stakeholder Pensions were capped for the first ten years. A random search on the internet of funds available in Self Invested Personal Pensions produces many similar results.

11 An example would be audit fees, i.e. what the fund pays accountants to check that its figures are correct.

12 The visible cost of buying and selling shares includes commissions and taxes.

13 The invisible cost of buying and selling shares includes the fractional mark-up and discount that portfolio managers incur when they buy and sell shares, respectively, in the market.

14 As per an informal survey by the authors; see also Kevin James, 'The Price of Retail Investing in the UK', FSA, February 2000, p. 34.

15 In the US, for example, the headline expense figure that fund managers disclose is equivalent to the UK's total expense ratio (TER).

16 Informal author survey of equity funds run by two big UK retail fund managers (M&G and Jupiter). Note that these Reduction in Yield figures assume that investors do actually pay initial and/or exit charges, i.e. they do not receive any kind of rebate.

17 The chief executive of the Investment Management Association (IMA), in a letter to the *Financial Times* on 4 December 2009. He also admitted in his letter that even insiders 'were surprised to discover that the information was less easy to track down than we had supposed'. Interestingly, Canadian regulators now require funds to disclose a 'Trading Expense Ratio' that captures visible trading costs. This appears in a relatively prominent position (the Manager's Report on Fund Performance).

18 Implied by Kevin James, 'The Price of Retail Investing in the UK', Financial Services Authority, February 2000. Our figure divides James's 'cost of a round-trip trade' (page 23) into visible and invisible components. On page 47, James

estimates combined 'trading costs' (using our terminology: both visible and invisible) at between 1.05 and 1.60 per cent per annum.

19 All these figures assume inflation is always zero, i.e. they are in real (as well as in nominal) terms. The annual return of five per cent per annum is purely an illustrative figure based on long-term returns in the stock market.

20 The average balance during the first year is slightly more than £900, which at 1.5 per cent produces a fee of about £15.

21 This is because the pot has grown substantially. Every year it has received another nine per cent of Colin's (rising) salary, as well as getting five per cent growth from its investments.

22 The other one is annuity rates, whatever they turn out to be in 2051.

23 This is not very surprising when you consider that the 1.5 per cent per annum Colin has been paying in charges is a bit less than one-third of the five per cent per annum his investments were earning. By far the most sensible way to think about the costs of investing is to compare them with the return you expect to earn. Thus, Colin should compare his 1.5 per cent costs to his five per cent return (remember always to subtract inflation from any return you expect to make).

24 This is not fantasy. NEST (see chapter 5) will manage millions of people's pension funds for 0.3 per cent annum. Other large company schemes are also able to use their scale to deliver annual charges well below one per cent.

25 This is a slight simplification because it ignores any 'tracking error', positive or negative.

26 Murthi, Orszag and Orszag, 'Administrative Costs under a Decentralized Approach to Individual Accounts: Lessons from the United Kingdom', 2001.

27 Murthi, Orszag and Orszag, 2001.

28 Murthi, Orszag and Orszag, 2001: 'Those purchasing annuities are likely to have longer life expectancies than the general population—both because of socioeconomic reasons and because of individual behaviour... This adverse selection effect means that if someone with the typical life expectancy wishes to purchase an annuity, he or she must pay a premium relative to the actuarial fair price' (page 325). In other words, if you have to buy an annuity to cover your retirement (because you belonged to a DC scheme rather than a DB scheme), you will be penalised relative to the income you would have received in a DB scheme. See also Michael Johnson, 'Simplification is the Key', Centre for Policy Studies, 2010, p. 23.

29 *Daily Telegraph*, 11 June 2010.

3: How Did We Get Here?

1 Surveys by the insurance company Aviva suggest that people hope to retire with around 70 per cent of their pre-retirement income. Most will in fact receive 30 per cent or less.

2 The attitude of many Members of Parliament, and a substantial portion of the electorate, was summed up by Frederick Millar, Secretary of the Liberty and Property League, in a pamphlet on pensions published in 1903: 'Pauperism is not to be fought by inviting large numbers of persons who are independent of state aid to become dependent on it.'

3 The Labour Party, which advocated a state pension, was growing fast: the Liberals were able to form a majority in the

Commons after the election in 1910 only by agreeing to a coalition with Labour.

4   Two candidates to be identified as the UK's first occupational pension scheme are the Royal Navy's Chatham Chest (1590), which can still be viewed—the original chest, that is—in the museum at Chatham Dockyard; and a Customs and Excise scheme started in 1671. The East India Company created its own pension scheme a century later. The Institute of Actuaries—actuaries work out how long people are likely to live, a calculation critical for any pension scheme—was founded in 1848.

5   Office for National Statistics, 'Occupational Pension Schemes Survey', 2009, p. 9. This figure does not include public sector employees contributing to occupational schemes.

6   We have been unable to track down DB contribution levels that prevailed in the 1970s, but it is safe to say they were lower than they are now. As recently as 2000, the average DB pension contribution was 16.2% of salary (5.0% employee, 11.2% employer)—Government Actuary's Department, 'Occupational pension schemes 2000'. Table 1 shows that today's figure is 21.6% (4.9% employee, 16.6% employer).

7   Quoted in *The Economist*, 15 May, 1999, p. 116. The actuary was referring to American and German DB schemes, but British DB schemes were no different in this respect.

8   *The Lawyer*, 10 June 2002.

9   Ian Drury, *Daily Mail*, 3 November 2008.

10 Alex Brummer, 'The man who stole your old age: How Gordon Brown secretly imposed a ruinous tax that has wrecked the retirement of millions', *Daily Mail*, 16 April, 2010.

11 Evan Davis, available at
http://www.bbc.co.uk/blogs/thereporters/evandavis/2007/04/
that_pensions_raid.html

12 One of the most cogent expressions of what the Thatcherite
Conservatives aimed to do is Nigel Lawson's lecture 'The
New Conservatism', delivered to the Bow Group, 4 August,
1980. It is reprinted in his *The View from No 11*, and can also
be accessed at
http://www.margaretthatcher.org/document/109505

13 In an interview with *Woman's Own,* 31 October, 1987. The
full transcript is available at
http://www.margaretthatcher.org/document/106689. In 1979,
in a draft for a speech at the Conservative Party Conference,
she had written 'There is no such thing as a collective
conscience, collective kindness, collective gentleness,
collective freedom'. See *An Early Draft of Mrs Thatcher's 'No
such thing as society',* Tom Baldwin, *The Times,* 30 January,
2010.

14 Mrs Thatcher echoed the American philosopher Robert
Nozick, who had written in *Anarchy, State and Utopia,* pp. 32-
33: 'Individually, we each sometimes choose to undergo
some pain or sacrifice for a greater benefit or to avoid a
greater harm: [for instance] some people save money to
support themselves when they are older... Why not,
similarly, hold that some persons have to bear some cost that
benefits other persons more, for the sake of the overall social
good? But there is no *social entity* with a good that undergoes
some sacrifice for its own good. There are only individual
people, different individual people, with their own
individual lives. Using one of these people for the benefit of
others, uses him and benefits the others. Nothing more.
What happens is that something is done to him for the sake
of the others. Talk of an overall social good covers this up.'

15 Norman Fowler, *Ministers Decide: A Personal Memoir of the Thatcher Years*, London: Chapmans, 1991, pp. 203-224.

16 Nigel Lawson, *The View from Number 11*, p. 590. Pages 587-592 of the book relate, with Lawson's characteristic clarity and verve, his successful campaign to defeat compulsory personal pensions. Norman Fowler sees what happened rather differently, writing: 'As long as I live I will regret having to abandon our plans to give an occupational pension to very worker in the country. It was the worst decision that I had ever to take in Government. That is not to say it was the wrong decision. Given the position in November 1985, there was no other decision for a politician to take.' He blames Nigel Lawson for that situation. See *Ministers Decide, A Personal Memoir of the Thatcher Years*, p. 222.

17 Lawson, *The View from Number 11*, p. 591.

18 SERPS would eventually be abolished by Tony Blair in 2002.

19 Essentially because the Conservatives decided that they had to give people who took out personal pensions the right to go back into SERPS—and that proved to be very expensive. See David Blake, 'Two decades of pension reform in the UK: what are the implications for occupational pensions?' Pensions Institute, Cass Business School, March 2000; available at http://www.pensions-institute.org/

20 Blake, 'Two decades of pension reform in the UK', p. 227.

21 Edward Whitehouse, 'Pension reform, financial literacy and public information: a case study of the United Kingdom', World Bank, January 2000, p. 18. It is important to note that an individual can (and often does) have more than one personal pension plan, so the number of individuals involved may well have been less than 5.7 million.

22 But that was not how it appeared to the ministers responsible for the changes. For years, they remained convinced that—as Norman Fowler wrote in 1991—'in many ways the most spectacular success has been the new pension options. Over four million people have taken out personal pensions. Over 800,000 people are now covered by new occupational pension schemes [...] The public have been provided with more choices, and have shown that they want a pension which is theirs by right [...] The case for abolishing SERPS altogether and for second pensions to be provided by funded schemes in the private sector remains powerful.' *Ministers Decide: A Personal Memoir of the Thatcher Years*, p. 224.

23 Laurie Dennett, *A Sense of Security: 150 years of the Prudential*, Granta, 1998, p. 372.

24 Dennett, *A Sense of Security*, p. 372.

25 Financial Services Authority, 28 January 2002.

26 Blake, 'Two decades of pension reform in the UK', p. 227.

27 Whitehouse, 'Pension reform, financial literacy and public information: a case study of the United Kingdom', January 2000.

28 Financial Services Authority, 1 December 2000.

29 Philip Booth denies this, in 'Britain's pension problem: government failure', *Freeman*, May 2005, Vol. 5, issue 4; and *The Way out of the Pension Quagmire*, Institute of Economic Affairs, 2005. He claims that 'the entire pension mis-selling debacle arose as a result, not of privatisation, but of government interference with private employment contracts'. His argument for this surprising conclusion is bizarre. He states that people were 'enticed into leaving company schemes to take out personal pensions' when the government 'removed from privately negotiated employment contracts the clauses

that had required employees to join company pension schemes'. Precisely how the Government's decision to permit individuals to opt out of company schemes could have caused financial intermediaries to sell those people who took up the option pensions that were clearly unsuitable for them is obscure.

30 'Pyrrhic Victory? The unintended consequences of the Pensions Act 2004', Report in 2005 from the Pensions Institute, Cass Business School.

31 The technically inclined will appreciate we are simplifying here by ignoring the time value of money.

32 PPI, 'Pension Facts', October 2010, Table 20.

33 Source: PPF 7800 Index. NB: this calculation uses yet another technical basis for calculating the value of pension promises, but the broad pattern would be similar under FRS 17.

34 Con Keating's 'Don't stop thinking about tomorrow: the future of pensions', *Long Finance*, 2010, contains an impassioned and intriguing statement of the case 'against'.

4: Why We Make Bad Choices on Pensions

1 We take this to be the model that free markets are efficient. This can be expressed in various ways. Economists have found the various elaborations of mathematical proofs of the 'fundamental theorem of welfare economics' seductive; politicians like to emphasise the practical benefits of freedom, and the market's price mechanism. Rather than use mathematical models, they point to the undeniable failure of socialist and collectivist economies to deliver the prosperity of the capitalist ones based on individual choice.

2 Pensions Commission, Report, 2004, has a detailed discussion of the savings rate in the UK. Cited by Johnson,

P. *et al.*, 'Making automatic enrolment work', Dept for Work and Pensions, October 2010.

3   Ruth Hancock, *et al.*, 'Projections of owner-occupation rates, house values, income and financial assets among older people, UK, 2002-2022', Personal Social Services Research Unit, Discussion Paper 2373.

4   See pp. 62-63 of this report, which provides the appropriate references.

5   Professor Tim Congdon, in 'The Pension Commission: is Adair Turner irrational or confused?', *Economic Affairs*, March 2005, has produced a novel variation on this idea. He claims that it is just wrong to suggest that people have been saving less for their retirement. It is rather that, instead of saving in pension funds, they have been saving by buying their homes—an investment strategy which, he claims, is a rational way of providing for old age. But while people *could* have bought their primary residence in order to be able to sell it and use the proceeds to provide a pension, there is no evidence that they have in fact done so. Professor Congdon does not provide any data to show that most people see a home primarily as an asset to be sold to provide a pension, rather than as a living space to which they are sentimentally attached and where they want to live in for as long as possible. The value of property is also liable to collapses at least as extreme as those of the stock market. It is far from certain that investing in property is, over the long term, a rational bet.

6   HSBC has published a series of reports on what people want and expect from later life, ageing and retirement: see for example *The Future of Retirement: the new old age*, based on interviews with 20,000 people aged 40-79. The report can be found at : http://www.hsbc.com/ 1/PA_1_1_S5/content/assets/retirement/2008_for_report.pdf

7   Joseph Stiglitz makes this point in *Freefall*, p. 249: 'At the end of your life, you might say: I wish I had saved more—the last years have been really painful, I would willingly have given up one of my earlier beach vacations to have had some more spending money today. Or you might say: I wish I had saved less. I could have enjoyed the money so much more when I was younger. Either way, you can't go back and relive your life... Accordingly, it's not clear what economists really mean when they try to extend the model of rationality that applies to choices among flavours of ice cream to... how you invest your saving for your retirement.'

8   According to Edward Whitehouse: *Pension Reform, Financial Literacy and Public Education: A Case Study of the United Kingdom*, 15 per cent of those who start a personal pension drop out after one year; and 40 per cent of those who took out a personal pension in 1993 were not contributing to one four years later.

9   One MORI poll suggests that four out of five people do not even know what APR stands for, let alone how to calculate it accurately. See http://www.credithelpline.net/personal_debt_stats.html. Lauren E. Willis, *Against Financial Literary Education*, Iowa Law Review, 94, 2008, has a good summary of evidence from America on just how limited most people's mathematical skills are.

10 A survey by the Skipton Building Society reported that winning the National Lottery is a significant part of the financial planning of one in seven Yorkshire residents. That's an extreme example of over-optimism, but there is a general tendency to over-estimate the probability of favourable events. A NatWest survey in 2008 of 8,500 teenagers in the UK found that the expected on average to be earning a salary of £31,000 at the age of 25. In reality, 22-

29 year olds in the UK earn on average £17,817. For evidence that over-optimism is a characteristic of normal human thought, see Ellen J. Langer and Jane Roth, 'Heads I win, Tails it's chance', *Journal of Personality and Social Psychology* 32(6), 951-955.

11 MORI, 'Savers Struck with Apathy and Confusion', quoted in Edward Whitehouse: *Pension Reform, Financial Literacy and Public Education: A Case Study of the United Kingdom,* January 2000, available online at http://mpra.ub.uni-muenchen.de/10323/

12 Although by no means all. See Gabaix, Xavier and Laibson, David, 'Shrouded Attributes, Consumer Myopia, and Information Suppression in Competitive Markets', MIT Dept of Economics Working Paper 05-18.

13 Gabaix and Laibson, 'Shrouded Attributes, Consumer Myopia, and Information Suppression in Competitive Markets'.

14 They also show why the same phenomenon happens with several other products and services, including computer printers and hotel rooms.

15 In one HSBC Pension Plan, for instance, £120,000 paid in over 40 years would result in fees and commissions totalling £99,900. Revealingly, HSBC claims its fees are 'competitive with the rest of the industry'. Panorama, *Who's Taken My Pension?* BBC 1, broadcast on 4 October 2010.

16 David de Meza, Bernd Irlenbusch and Diane Reyniers, 'Financial capability: a behavioural economics perspective', FSA Consumer Research 69, July, 2008, has a very useful survey of the repeated irrationalities in decision-making that have been identified, with references—although some of the items referred to in the text are not listed in the bibliography at the end.

17 Terrance Odean provides an analysis of the deleterious effects of one variety of optimism—overconfidence in one's own judgement to pick and trade stocks profitably—in 'Volume, volatility, price and profit when all traders are above average', *The Journal of Finance*, Vol. 53, No. 6, December, 1998, pp. 1887-1934.

18 Financial advisers and salespeople who were responsible for the £12 billion pensions mis-selling scandal behaved in a fashion parallel to doctors recommending unnecessary or dangerous treatment. It is arguable that many advisers today who recommend high-cost managed funds as the best pension investment are doing the same.

19 The explanation for the widening gap between average pay and the pay of top executives may be similar. In 1980, in the US, top CEOs earned an average of 42 times the amount the average worker was paid. In 2001, they made 531 times as much. CEOs could have paid themselves 531 times the average salary in 1980. Why didn't they? Possibly because in 1980, CEOs did not think they were worth 531 times more than ordinary workers: they had not had 20 years of economists and politicians telling them that their only responsibility was to maximize their own self interest, and if they did that, they would benefit everyone else to the greatest possible extent.

20 Dan Ariely, *Predictably Irrational: the Hidden Forces that Shape our Decisions*, London: Harpercollins, 2009, pp. 195-216.

21 Throughout this report the word 'intermediary' is used generically, rather than in any technical legal or regulatory sense it may have in the UK. That is, it refers to people or organisations who mediate in any capacity between individuals and their investments.

22 Financial Services Authority, 'Public understanding of financial services: a strategy for consumer education', Consultation Paper no. 15, London, 1998.

23 This is very clearly shown in Edward Whitehouse's 2000 survey of the failure of FSA's attempts to improve financial decisions by providing consumers with more information.

24 Pensions Policy Institute, 'Retirement income and assets: outlook for the future', February 2010.

25 Alan Greenspan, 'Consumer Finance', lecture at the Federal Reserve System's Fourth Annual Community Affairs Research Conference, Washington, DC, 8 April 2005.

26 He also assumed that the people who ran the banks knew what they were doing—an assumption that, in his Congressional testimony on 23 October 2008, he had to admit had been shown to be false. 'Those of us who looked to the self-interest of lending institutions to protect shareholder's equity (myself especially) are in a state of shocked disbelief.'

27 'Against financial literacy', *Iowa Law Review*, 94, 2008.

28 The Consumer Fraud Research Group, NASD Investor Education Foundation, Investor Fraud Study Final Report 5 (2006). The high level of financial competence of those who fell victim to Bernard Madoff (which included the managers of Harvard University's investment fund) supports that finding.

29 de Meza, Irlenbusch and Reyniers, *Financial Capability*, 2008.

30 The Treasury, on the other hand, to judge from the report by Otto Thorensen published in March 2008, maintains the view that better information is all that is required for the 'rational choice' model to work and produce the optimal results for everyone that the theory predicts it will.

31 The classic paper is Cass R. Sunstein and Richard H. Thaler, 'Liberal Paternalism is not an Oxymoron', May 2003; http://www.law.uchicago.edu/Lawecon/index.html. It was followed by their book *Nudge: Improving Decisions About Health, Wealth and Happiness*, Yale, 2008. The ideas have been enthusiastically embraced by the present government: there is even a 'nudge unit' attached to the Prime Minister's office. It investigates how to design policies that will take advantage of the behavioural biases that Sunstein and Thaler have identified.

32 Hargreaves Lansdown, 'Self Invested Personal Pensions — the commonsense way to build a pension'. No date, but sent out in 2010.

33 FT Investment Adviser, 18 October 2010 and 25 October 2010.

34 HMRC data.

35 The term 'intermediary' is used generically.

36 Hargreaves Lansdown, 'Self Invested Personal Pensions — the commonsense way to build a pension'. No date, but sent out in 2010.

37 AJ Bell's annual reports are available at www.ajbell.co.uk

38 AJ Bell's annual report, 2007, p. 7.

39 FT Investment Adviser, 25 October 2010.

40 HMRC data.

41 Occupational Pensions Defence Union Report 25, November 2008.

42 FSA, 'Quality of advice on pension switching — a report on the findings of a thematic review', December 2008. The quote comes from a 5 December press release about the report.

43 Hargreaves Lansdown website;
http://www.h-l.co.uk/pensions/sipp/sipp2

44 Killik & Co, 'SIPPs explained—how to plan for your
retirement', no date, accessed November 2010.

45 Reuters, 28 May 2008. Cuthbert, who works for an
independent firm, appears to be hinting that a different
group of players—insurance companies—are the worst
offenders.

46 FSA, 'Quality of advice on pension switching – a report on
the findings of a thematic review', December 2008. The
quote comes from a 5 December press release about the
report.

47 FSA, 'Quality of advice on pension switching – a report on
the findings of a thematic review', December 2008, p. 4.

48 Quotes and details from the previously cited FSA report.

49 See FSA publications at
http://www.fsa.gov.uk/pages/Library/Communication/PR/2
011/024.shtml and
http://www.fsa.gov.uk/pages/Library/Other_publications/pe
nsion_switching/index.shtml

50 Available at http://www.fsa.gov.uk/pubs/final/awd.pdf

51 Data on AWD Chase de Vere comes from FSA publications
and from the accounts of AWD Chase de Vere's UK parent,
AWD Group plc, which are available at
www.companieshouse.gov.uk

52 The others were: Cricket Hill Financial Planning Ltd,
Perspective Financial Management, RSM Tenon Financial
Services Limited, Financial Limited, Robin Bradford (Life
and Pension Consultants) Ltd and N-Hanced LLP. See note
49 above.

53 In the Penalty Notice; available at
   http://www.fsa.gov.uk/pubs/final/awd.pdf

54 Patrick Connolly of AWD Chase de Vere, quoted in *Money
   Observer*, 17 November 2010. Available at
   http://newpf.iii.co.uk/articles/articledisplay.jsp?article_id=10
   122270&section=Planning

55 Tom McPhail of Hargreaves Lansdown, quoted in the *Daily
   Telegraph*, 23 January 2008.

5: What Next?

1 Don Ezra, 'Defined-benefit and defined-contribution plans
  of the future', *Financial Analysts Journal*, Vol. 63, No. 1, 2007.

2 See, for example, Adair Turner, 'Reforming finance: are we
  being radical enough?', Clare Distinguished Lecture in
  Economics and Public Policy, February 18, 2011.

3 Alternatively, if you use a sufficiently anaemic notion of
  'rational', it is no doubt possible to claim that the situation
  had the structure of the Prisoners' Dilemma: the option
  chosen by each individual was rational, but it led to an
  outcome that was disastrous for everyone. This leads to
  well-known paradoxes about whether individual choices
  with that collective result can count as 'rational'.

4 Pensions Policy Institute, 'Retirement income and assets:
  outlook for the future', February 2010; chart 12, p. 35.

5 The evidence from America shows that if people have to
  make a decision to opt out, most of them won't do so —
  which means they will start saving. See Cass R. Sunstein and
  Richard H. Thaler 'Liberal Paternalism is not an Oxymoron'
  May 2003;
  http://www.law.uchicago.edu/Lawecon/index.html
  and *Nudge*, 2008.

6 *Japan Times*, 'Special Panel to Investigate Pensions Fiasco', 9 June, 2007.

7 Paul Johnson, David Yeandle and Adrian Boulding, 'Making automatic enrolment work', DWP, October 2010.

8 Mamta Murthi, J. Michael Orszag, and Peter R., Orszag, 'Administrative Costs under a Decentralized Approach to Individual Accounts: Lessons from the United Kingdom', World Bank, 2001.

9 See for example the Hutton Report and Michael Johnson's reports for the CPS.

10 List at Michael Johnson, 'Self-sufficiency is the key', Centre for Policy Studies, London: February 2011, pp. 58-59.

11 Changes in accounting rules would also probably be necessary. See Con Keating's report 'Don't stop thinking about tomorrow: the future of pensions', *Long Finance*, 2010.